Behind
the
Book

Chicago Guides
to Writing, Editing,
and Publishing

The Chicago Guide to Fact-Checking
Brooke Borel

Writing Abroad
Peter Chilson and Joanne B. Mulcahy

Immersion
Ted Conover

The Architecture of Story
Will Dunne

Character, Scene, and Story
Will Dunne

The Dramatic Writer's Companion
Will Dunne

The Business of Being a Writer
Jane Friedman

The Art of Creative Research
Philip Gerard

Getting It Published
William Germano

What Editors Do
Peter Ginna, editor

Storycraft
Jack Hart

A Poet's Guide to Poetry
Mary Kinzie

The Subversive Copy Editor
Carol Fisher Saller

The Writer's Diet
Helen Sword

Behind the Book

*Eleven Authors on Their
Path to Publication*

Chris Mackenzie Jones

The University of Chicago Press
Chicago and London

The University of Chicago Press, Chicago 60637
The University of Chicago Press, Ltd., London
Published 2018
Printed in the United States of America

27 26 25 24 23 22 21 20 19 18   1 2 3 4 5

ISBN-13: 978-0-226-40577-3 (cloth)
ISBN-13: 978-0-226-40580-3 (paper)
ISBN-13: 978-0-226-40594-0 (e-book)

DOI: https://doi.org/10.7208/chicago/[9780226405940].001.0001

Library of Congress Cataloging-in-Publication Data
Names: Jones, Chris Mackenzie, author.
Title: Behind the book : eleven authors on their path to publication /
Chris Mackenzie Jones.
Other titles: Chicago guides to writing, editing, and publishing.
Description: Chicago ; London : The University of Chicago Press, 2018. |
Series: Chicago guides to writing, editing, and publishing
Identifiers: LCCN 2017056780 | ISBN 9780226405773 (cloth : alk. paper) |
ISBN 9780226405803 (pbk. : alk. paper) | ISBN 9780226405940 (e-book)
Subjects: LCSH: Authors and publishers. | Authorship. | Editing.
Classification: LCC PN155 .J654 2018 | DDC 808.02—dc23
LC record available at https://lccn.loc.gov/2017056780

♾ This paper meets the requirements of ANSI/NISO Z39.48-1992
(Permanence of Paper).

Contents

The Brief Lineup   1

The Ignored Question: How   5

1: Sparks of Story   12

2: Processing Process   32

3: Sources of Support   47

4: Craft Quandaries   63

5: Thorough Themes   79

6: Reviewing Revision   92

7: Publishing Paths   116

8: Setbacks and Perseverance   137

9: Preparing to Publish   150

10: The Book in the World   163

11: Lessons Learned   178

Acknowledgments   195   *Appendix: The Complete Lineup*   197

Notes   211   *Index*   215

The Brief Lineup

For further details about the books, please refer to the appendix.

Clara Bensen, *No Baggage: A Minimalist Tale of Love and Wandering*
Genre: travel memoir
Publisher: Running Press, a member of the Perseus Books Group
Publication year: 2016
Time from idea to publication: 8 months
Editor: Jennifer Kasius
Agent: Stacy Testa

Brian Benson, *Going Somewhere: A Bicycle Journey across America*
Genre: narrative nonfiction (memoir)
Publisher: Plume, an imprint of Penguin Random House
Publication year: 2014
Time from idea to publication: 5 years
Editor: Denise Roy
Agent: David Forrer

Cynthia Bond, *Ruby*
Genre: literary fiction
Publisher: Hogarth, an imprint of Penguin
    Random House
Publication year: 2014
Time from idea to publication: 15 years
Editor: Lindsay Sagnette
Agent: Nicole Aragi

Delilah Dawson, *Wicked as They Come*
Genre: paranormal romance
Publisher: Pocket Books, a division of Simon & Schuster
Publication year: 2012
Time from idea to publication: 2 years
Editor: Abby Zidle
Agent: Kate McKean

Zetta Elliott, *Bird*
Genre: children's picture book
Publisher: Lee & Low Books
Publication year: 2008
Time from idea to publication: 5 years
Editor: Louise May
Agent: none

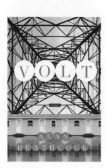

Alan Heathcock, *Volt*
Genre: short stories
Publisher: Graywolf Press
Publication year: 2011
Time from idea to publication: 10 years
Editor: Fiona McCrae
Agent: Sarah Burnes

Edan Lepucki, *California*
Genre: postapocalyptic literary fiction
Publisher: Little, Brown, an imprint of Hachette
Publication year: 2014
Time from idea to publication: 4 years
Editor: Allie Sommer
Agent: Erin Hosier

Rebecca Makkai, *The Borrower*
Genre: literary fiction
Publisher: Viking, an imprint of Penguin Random House
Publication year: 2011
Time from idea to publication: 10 years
Editor: Alexis Washam
Agent: Nicole Aragi

Courtney Maum, *I Am Having So Much Fun Here*
without You
Genre: literary fiction
Publisher: Touchstone, an imprint of Simon and Schuster
Publication year: 2014
Time from idea to publication: 12 years
Editor: Sally Kim
Agent: Rebecca Gradinger

Eric Smith, *Inked*
Genre: young adult fantasy
Publisher: Bloomsbury Spark, a young adult digital
    imprint of Bloomsbury Publishing
Publication year: 2015
Time from idea to publication: 3 years
Editor: Meredith Rich
Agent: Dawn Frederick

Monona Wali, *My Blue Skin Lover*
Genre: magical realism, literary fiction
Publisher: Blue Jay Ink
Publication year: 2014
Time from idea to publication: 4 years
Editor: none
Agent: none

The Ignored Question: How

For almost as long as people have existed, we've told stories. Legends, myths, oral and recorded histories — it's an ancient and modern art, and a uniquely human experience.

Brain studies reveal that not only are we hard-wired to receive stories, but our brains don't differentiate between real and read experiences. Amazingly, they register identically in brain scans.[1]

At its most basic, story is a survival instinct. The brain craves it, using stories to explore uncharted paths and to strategize new experiences from the safety of the imagination.

But though the craving of story is hard-wired, the crafting of it isn't as simple.

Why We Write

For centuries, and across distant and disconnected cultures, philosophers have asked questions around why we tell stories. Aristotle in the Western tradition[2] and Confucius in the Eastern[3] both spent significant time discussing the reasons behind storytelling.

In more modern times, writers continue to grapple with these questions. In George Orwell's famous 1946 essay "Why I Write," he named ego, aesthetics, posterity, and politics as the four driving forces behind his work.[4] Many years later Joan Didion, in an essay with the same title, challenged Orwell's assumptions and said that the act of self-expression is what drives her writing.[5]

Across all genres, with an almost endless number of writers weighing in, this conversation continues. In his famous poem "Ars Poetica," Archibald Macleish argues that we write for art's sake: "a poem should not mean / But be."[6]

In her now celebrated lecture "The Devil Girl from Mars," Octavia Butler admits that she was driven to tell stories after she saw a bad movie and knew she could do better.[7]

Some writers even claim storytelling is out of their control. In the excellent book *Why We Write: 20 Acclaimed Authors on How and Why They Do What They Do*, the thriller writer David Baldacci says that for him writing is a compulsion, and that if writing were illegal, he'd just go to jail.[8] Others do not claim this level of obsession but still feel compelled by their need to tell stories.

I work at The Loft Literary Center in Minneapolis, a leading literary arts center in the United States, and in my time there I've met many aspiring storytellers and writers. The reasons to write are as varied as the people who write, and involve a complicated stew of ego, ambition, connection, expression, art, delusion, posterity, emotional need, obsession, and challenge.

But the essays, interviews, and Q&As about why we write don't usually address how we make it happen. The reasons we write are personal and varied, and writers discuss them endlessly. *How* we write is a simpler question; however, for some reason it often goes unasked and unexplored.

The stories in this book will help us consider the question of *how* we write, which does not mean the physical process—how to set up a writing space, what time of day to write, how many words to get down at a time, whether to use pen or keyboard. Instead we'll explore how our urge to write, wherever it originates, moves from desire to reality. The how isn't more important than the why, but it does have higher personal stakes: Either we figure it out and publish, or we never get past the idea stage and our work or idea remains stymied and unshared.

In this book we'll go beyond urge and get to urgency and its fruition. Through eleven examples, we'll explore the path of the successful debut author and the life history of their first book. I will weave together their experiences into a composite picture showing how process became publication, how an idea became a first book.

Why These Books?

Two weeks after signing the contract for this book, I was diagnosed with an aggressive form of skin cancer. It changed everything about the book's publication path. The medical procedures, appointments, and uncertainty became part of it. Apart from this paragraph, you'd be entirely unaware that cancer diagnosis and treatment have affected my writing, yet they've been stitched into this book's unique DNA.

My author interviews have revealed that some level of background noise seeps into the making of every published book: a series of challenging circumstances that could never be intentionally replicated, and that most readers would be oblivious to. If my own experience and these eleven profiles demonstrate anything, it's that there's no one way to bring a book into the world, and that replicating another author's path is neither possible nor necessary. You will form your own path.

So if the stories are varied and each path is unique, why write this book? Aren't these one-off anecdotes, maybe gratifying and important to the authors themselves but not useful to anyone else?

This isn't as much of a conundrum as it sounds. Because while no path can be completely replicated, each can be explored and mined for substantial lessons. Each of us will need to reconfigure tactics for our own process, but we can and should learn by example from as many people as we can.

In Lisa Cron's 2012 book *Wired for Story*, we learn that the human brain's craving for story is part of a neurological need to try on new lives and new situations.[9] We can empathize and learn from a ship captain obsessed with a whale even if we've never seen a whale, a ship, or the ocean. As aspiring writers, we can learn lessons from unique approaches and circumstances. That's the theory behind this book—my hope is that any aspiring writer will find these stories valuable.

It's also true that this book would be quite different if it profiled eleven other authors. But that doesn't mean it's a random collection of stories. These books and authors weren't selected with a dartboard. I started this project by prioritizing a few important aspects of debut books: recentness, breadth, and results.

I selected debut books published in the last several years to best connect this book to the contemporary first-time author. There would undoubtedly be value in examining the decisions behind literary classics or in profiling an accomplished writer pulling together her tenth novel, but in both cases the examples would be less relevant to a first-time author. I've chosen examples that shed light on the challenges and questions involved in trying to bring a first book into today's ever-shifting publishing landscape.

I also sought authors and books that represent a wide breadth of genres, backgrounds, approaches, styles, and goals. The eleven featured books are on a wide gamut of genres and styles, including a short story collection, literary fiction, speculative fiction, paranormal romance, magical realism, narrative nonfiction, memoir, young adult fantasy, and children's picture book. While this scope is broad, it does exclude poetry, screenwriting, researched nonfiction, and scholarly texts, among others. I have a lot of respect and love for those types of excluded books (I cut my teeth in the University of Florida's MFA poetry program). But these genres are so different in craft and publishing approach that it felt like a disservice to try force them to share these pages side by side.

And finally, I chose these eleven authors based on the results of their first books. By one measure or another, each of these books can be called a successful debut. That doesn't mean just runaway best sellers (though some of them are). I looked at success through a number of different lenses, taking into account critical attention, honors and awards, sales, subsequent projects, achieving personal goals, or some combination of them all.

Once recruited, the authors generously gave me a considerable amount of their time. I interviewed them, sometimes multiple times. In many cases I also interviewed key people involved in their projects: their agents, editors, and support networks.

Why This Book Is Different from Other Books about Writing

There are dozens of fantastic books that cover the craft and publishing sides of writing. There are troves of online publications, blogs, videos, and interviews, all dedicated to these topics. And as we've just explored, there is a varied and rich, centuries-old conversation around why we choose to write.

This book covers many craft, publishing, and business decisions faced by the eleven debut authors. Through their stories we'll gain insights for our own writing process and approach. If you're seeking a step-by-step manual for specific questions of craft or publishing, though, there are excellent resources already out there. This book does not attempt to repeat or improve upon them.

I mention those resources when relevant, but I focus on a different goal—exploring the paths that successful modern authors take to birth their first book. I'll certainly address questions of craft and publication, but the path will be highlighted more than the end result. With "how?" as our guiding question, we can widen our lens to examine the full story behind publishing a first book.

In my time at the Loft, I've met thousands of storytellers. Some call themselves writers; some fear that title. They come to the Loft with different reasons, goals, aspirations, and expectations. Some are timid, some are confident, but they almost always share two traits: a desire to write and a doubt about doing it.

Some feel unqualified or unready. They don't feel like they belong in the same room as people who call themselves writers. Some have an idea but aren't sure where or how to begin. Others may have confidence in their writing—some have written for years and have published in numerous journals or online venues—but the changing landscape of publishing is daunting. To them, it doesn't matter how good their story or prose is: they have no idea how it will get out into the world. Even the most advanced writers, confident in their skills to write and publish their first book, start to feel unsteady when approaching the less commonly explored sides of writing: the business, editorial, publicity, and publishing sides.

There are numerous resources available for these writers to educate and steady themselves, but few of those resources capture the whole timeline of a first book. How did the writer take that kernel of an idea all the way through the process to a successful book? Where did the author stumble or find resistance, and how did they get to the finish line? And with all the avenues and choices, is there even one answer anymore?

In this book we'll learn through example. We'll go along for the ride with eleven debut authors, exploring their diverse paths to publication. Each chapter will investigate these eleven books through the natural stages of book development: generating ideas, refining the focus, fostering support, polishing craft, building themes and structure, revising drafts, making a publishing choice, dealing with setbacks, preparing to publish, publishing, and moving on to the next project.

Though I'll avoid any hard-and-fast prescriptions, I hope to present enough options to reveal potential paths and tactics for other aspiring writers. Through these stories we'll come to better understand the possibilities and choices faced by the modern author.

The chapters in this book are organized by themes, and the authors' stories will weave in and out. With the exception of the first chapter, not every book or author will appear in every section; rather, I've chosen parts of various authors' writing and publishing journeys that are especially relevant to each theme.

These authors were kind enough to share their fears, their mistakes, their tips, their processes, and their ultimate lessons learned. Theirs aren't the only possible stories to tell, but they are powerful stories. So let's explore the multitude of paths. Let's go behind the books.

1. The Sparks of Story

Every book starts with the spark of a story. That spark might ignite quickly in a moment of genius or burn slowly for many years. Over time it may continue to fuel the project or fade to a smolder, but there's always something of that spark in the final flame of a published book.

It is, however, just the starting point. The fantasy author Patrick Rothfuss once encouraged writers to participate in National Novel Writing Month (NaNoWriMo) by blogging, "The worst unpublished novel of all-time is better than the brilliant idea you have in your head."[1] Anyone can say they have an idea for a book, but very few make the effort to follow through and write it. The spark will flicker out unless it's acted upon with skill and determination.

And yet for some reason, ideas are the most publicly revered part of the writing process. Read ten author interviews or attend ten author Q&As, and the question will come up at least nine times: Where did you come up with the idea for your book? The question suggests that prolific, successful writers have a kind of padlocked treasure chest of creativity, and if they'd just reveal the combination, we'd all be able to write the next best seller just like them.

In a 1997 essay, "Where Do You Get Your Ideas?," author Neil

Gaiman wrote that "the ideas aren't the hard bit."[2] Yet, as he explained, most successful authors face an all-too-common situation of being approached by a stranger with a can't-miss proposal. The details of the proposal vary, but the thrust is always the same: they'll do the hard part and tell you their brilliant book idea, and all you, the author, need to do is the easy part—write it all down.

A book cannot exist without an original impulse or inspiration. So it's important for writers to contemplate how other authors find and cultivate ideas for their work. Yet as Gaiman points out, the idea is only a small step in the process—and even with a great idea, it takes practice, skill, and hard work to make any book a reality. Many writers start out feeling the singular pressure of the idea—they feel stuck, uninspired, and lacking. The Muse has yet to visit, and so they wait.

As many of the debut authors profiled here demonstrate, that's usually not a successful approach. These eleven books have a variety of origin stories. They began in depression, outrage, disappointment, conversation, suggestion, romanticism, and dream. They were inspired by a note on a Paris door, the words of a twelfth-century poet, a journey around the world without bags, a trip across the United States on bikes, and nostalgia for New York prompted by the September 11 attacks. If these sparks of story have anything in common, it's in how the authors approached their ideas after they had them. Seeing how others found their ideas may help you spark one of your own, but the most important lesson here is that ideas need to be cultivated if they're to turn into anything concrete. Subsequent chapters will highlight the most compelling stories from our authors, skipping those that are quite similar. But to lay the groundwork and better introduce each book, this chapter covers every featured book's origin story.

Eric Smith's *Inked*

Eric Smith's *Inked* began, like most good stories, as a conversation. Eric lived in Philadelphia and worked in marketing for Quirk Books, a publisher with an eclectic collection of titles including *Miss Peregrine's Home for Peculiar Children*, *William Shakespeare's Star Wars Trilogy*, *The League of Regrettable Superheroes*, and *Pride and Prejudice and Zombies*. He also served as a contributor to several blogs and publications including *Bygone Bureau*, *Huffington Post*, and *BookRiot*.

One night Eric went out for beers with his "simply covered in ink" tattoo artist friend Brian. At the time Eric had self-published a book based on his graduate school work and "had a lot of other manuscripts in drawers." He'd started to explore a potential nonfiction book with Quirk, but he'd never contemplated writing a young adult novel.

Eric and Brian's conversation twisted and shifted, and at some point they turned to talking about the life of a tattoo artist. They talked about the ink, the machine, the wounds left after a fresh inking. Then they talked about the art. Just as a fitness instructor must be in shape, tattoo artists must have tattoos. Good ones. At least that's what Brian said. So they talked through Brian's tattoos, the ones he had, the ones he'd inked. Then Brian explained to Eric that with all the tattoos he'd received—all the ink in his life—there had been no question in his mind: he felt destined to become a tattoo artist.

"That stuck with me for a while," says Eric: "the concept of someone's tattoos setting them up for a future."

Predestination. Self-determination. Rebellion. Conformity. Mistakes. Tattoos could embody all of those ideas, sometimes conflicting ideas at the same time. This notion rattled around in Eric's mind. He didn't know what to make of it, but he couldn't shake it for several weeks.

No matter whether someone is drawn to or fearful of the mechanical prick of the needle, a tattoo is a powerful metaphor for choice. It's a permanent emblem or an intentional absence. Eric's friend Brian loved all of his ink and dedicated his working life to the art of inking others. Deep down, he believed that his tattoos might have determined his destiny. But in thinking about all the aspects of tattoos, a powerful question began to form in Eric's mind. What would happen if tattoos weren't a choice? And more, what would happen if people wanted something besides what was selected for them?

That question marked the moment *Inked* began. Eric didn't have characters or plot, but he had a world and a question. More than anything else, that question was what let Eric know that *Inked* would be a young adult novel. "It's an essential part of being a kid," says Eric. "You want to choose for yourself, but all around you there are people trying to choose for you. Parents, teachers, guidance counselors — and while they tend to mean well, it is irksome. Teens get a thrill out of the peer who does their own thing and goes against the grain."

Eric had his idea and his approach, and was ready to take the next steps in writing his book.

Rebecca Makkai's *The Borrower*

If a bar conversation started *Inked*, then outrage sparked Rebecca Makkai's *The Borrower*. In 2000 Rebecca had just graduated from Washington & Lee University. She has since gone on to become one of the most respected short-story writers in America, frequently publishing in places like *Harper's* magazine, *Tin House*, the *Wall Street Journal*, and *New England Review*. Her short stories were anthologized in *The Best American Short Stories* an impressive four years in a row (2008–11). Back in 2000, however, Rebecca had little publishing experience and was drafting short stories while teaching elementary school.

One day Rebecca read an article on gender rehabilitation programs for gay youth — children as young as six or seven — and it provoked a strong reaction. "It really affected me because I was teaching children around that age. I knew how impressionable and vulnerable and sensitive they are, but at the same time how fully formed these children were. I knew that someone asking them to change something so fundamental about themselves could really undo them for life," says Rebecca.

She remembers sharing her feelings about these programs with her mother. "And in a very Mom sort of way, she said, 'Oh, you should write a story about it.' And granted, that's her response to just about everything. You know, I'd get bronchitis and she'd say, 'Oh, you should write a story about that.'" But for some reason, this time the advice stuck a little more than usual. Rebecca started sketching out the idea.

Most of the time we read news stories passively. We might read about an oil spill, corporate fraud, or political corruption, but no matter what kind of emotion a story provokes, we're powerless to do much about it. As Rebecca read the story about gay rehabilitation programs, she realized it wasn't just outrage that she felt, it was the sense of being a powerless onlooker. But in her novel, instead of horror and apathy, she wanted to explore what would happen if helplessness turned into action. What if someone who had no right to do anything interfered in a dramatic way?

She felt she had a strong idea, but with no experience structuring a novel, Rebecca realized two things fairly quickly. First, this was not a short story; it did need to be a novel. And second, this was not the right time to write it. Like Gaiman in his essay, she quickly realized that "the ideas aren't the hard bit." So she set it aside.

Over the next several years, Rebecca tinkered with the manuscript from time to time but mostly focused on writing short stories, teaching full time, and starting her family. "At the time I saw myself eventually writing novels, but that seemed like such a huge, daunting, insane thing to do. I think I rightly intuited that you don't start writing a novel the instant you get an idea for it. These things need years to marinate." It would take several years before she turned her full attention back to *The Borrower* manuscript—a story I'll tell in a later chapter of this book.

Brian Benson's *Going Somewhere*

Brian Benson had never considered himself a writer before he rode his bike across the country with his girlfriend, Rachel. But the trip changed him, and he needed to make sense out of where he came from and where he was headed next. When he set out on the long trip, he did it for his girlfriend. "I'd decided to follow her anywhere, into anything," says Brian.

Rachel had suggested the trip, but halfway through—after hundreds of miles—something shifted in their relationship. They were starting to grow apart. But instead of resenting the trip, Brian came to see the journey as more about himself than about his dedication to her. Near the end of their journey, he realized their relationship might not last, but he'd found something he needed to explore. "When the idea came to me [to write the book], it was so vague and romantic and flowery that I didn't question it a lot," says Brian. "It wasn't so much about the bike trip when I was considering it originally; it was much more about choices."

Brian had mostly tamped down his creative side from childhood. He traces that back to elementary school. He and his sister Leah were placed in the same Gifted and Talented program, but they were separated into two different groups, he into the "intellectuals" and she into the "creatives." "Even then it felt like a silly distinction— we were both mainly making origami and building bridges out of toothpicks." He says he deeply internalized that split. For many years "Leah was the creative one, and I was the smart one," he says. "And I may not have known what 'being smart' meant, but I knew it didn't mean being creative."

On the long bike journey Brian began to rediscover his dormant creative side—drawing, journaling, and playing guitar. He had never written before—he'd never even considered it—but the trip allowed him to look at the world differently. He reviewed many stories from his life and made a decision that startled him: he wanted to write about the trip.

Few writers can point to a specific moment when they realized they wanted to write a book, but Brian can. He and Rachel were in Idaho, riding past a gas station on a heavily trafficked and highly potholed road. They were hot, hung over, and annoyed with each other, and still Brian remembers being really happy "in a way that didn't make any sense on the surface." For the first time in a long time, he felt a sense of purpose. "As I thought about it, these were the moments that resonated with the bigger questions I'd been asking. So the idea to write it came from a moment that was a mixture of adrenaline, inspiration, maybe low blood sugar, and a lack of self-awareness."

When Rachel and Brian reached their destination in Portland, Oregon—restless, weary, and hurt—he still had an overwhelming desire to write about the past several weeks. Days later he started writing, drawing on journal entries he'd made throughout the trip. "I don't think I considered in detail what it would be like to write a book with full character arcs and a deeper subtext and all those different dynamics. If I'd even had the language to consider all that, it would have terrified me, and I don't think I would have tried to write the book."

Brian didn't spend a lot of time considering it or letting it marinate, as some authors do. He plunged into writing the first page. "And it was the best first page written by anyone, ever, about anything," says Brian. "The next day I went back and reread that page and realized it was garbage." That realization led him to his next phase, giving up for quite a while.

Edan Lepucki's *California*

Many years before Stephen Colbert lifted Edan Lepucki's *California* in front of the cameras and encouraged his viewers to buy it, Edan had assigned a writing prompt to her students at Writing Workshops Los Angeles. She already had an idea for a "postapocalyptic domestic drama, basically a married couple at the end of the world." She says the spark for that idea came one day when she drove into downtown Los Angeles, noticed burned-out street lights, and wondered what it would look like if all the street lights stopped working.

In some ways, isn't this where many stories begin? Take an existing societal norm and just ask, what if this changed? While Edan was playing around with that idea, she assigned a new writing prompt to her class. The prompt was to write a scene in which a character interacts with a surprising secret object that he or she has hidden from other people for some reason. Edan had already developed some thoughts about the wife in her postapocalyptic story. But the secret object assignment crystallized her thinking and propelled her narrative forward. She started to write along with the class. She can't point to why she came up with a turkey baster as the secret object, but "that's kinda why I like writing exercises — you find whatever you can."

And if this wife would keep a turkey baster secret at the end of the world, what did that mean? Who was she? So Edan wrote about her a lot in class that day, about that turkey baster and what it meant to her. As she worked on that exercise, she didn't think she was working on her real manuscript. She just thought of it as a sketch for a down-the-road project that might never materialize. But then Edan had the rug pulled out from under her, and everything changed.

Edan had a draft of a manuscript titled "The Book of Deeds," and she'd just received a prestigious UCross artist's residency in Wyoming. She planned to use the residency to revise that manuscript based on her agent's notes. But about a week before she left, Edan's agent emailed her to say she couldn't sell the book and, furthermore, she didn't think she could represent Edan anymore. "My husband thought I had read an email that somebody had died, because I was shaking and suddenly crying," says Edan.

So she arrived at UCross with no agent and no manuscript to revise. Lost and defeated, and getting ready to abandon a book she'd worked on for five years, Edan returned to the writing she'd done for her class exercise. But this time she came with a different intention. "I wrote the beginning of *California* there, thinking, 'Nobody cares about me and nobody's ever going to see this.'"

Ten days into her residency, also influenced by an abandoned stone shelter on the grounds of that Wyoming ranch, Edan had written and revised forty pages of *California*. That was the most she'd ever written in such a short time.

For Edan, it wasn't one thing that jump-started her novel; instead an odd combination of disappointment, time to write, an abandoned building, a darkened street, a writing prompt, and a random secret turkey baster would form the foundation of *California*.

Courtney Maum's *I Am Having So Much Fun Here without You*

For Courtney Maum, *I Am Having So Much Fun Here without You* began with a note posted on a Paris door. She was living there and had just exited a difficult relationship. As much as Paris calls to other artists, Courtney says the perceived romance of the city and the failure of her relationship combined to stifle her creativity for quite some time.

As in Edan Lepucki's story, a period of darkness propelled Courtney to reconnect with her writing. But she struggled to find a way in. She spent a while looking for something to prompt her, and then one night she walked by a gallery on a familiar route. That night a note was attached to the door: "Dear Mr. Architect, you were wearing an elegant hat and you wanted to buy the blue bear. Please get in touch." That strange note would spark a dozen-year journey to publishing her debut novel.

Courtney's interest in the note didn't linger or seep in over time. It was instant. "'That's it,' I told myself. 'That's my prompt. What is this blue bear?'" She didn't have a story, she hadn't written in a long time, and she was not thinking this would become a novel. Instead she saw it as a prompt—a challenge and a way back into her creative process.

But as she considered this gallery and the architect, the blue bear became an image she couldn't release. What kind of painting would it be? Why would it be so important? And who would be buying it? Before she really noticed what she'd written, Courtney had started to construct a character and a novel around an unseen painting of a blue bear.

She would finish an entire draft of the manuscript fairly quickly, but after several setbacks and sidetracks which I'll cover in later chapters, Courtney put the manuscript away in a box. It had been an important story for her progress as a writer, but she abandoned it, certain it would never see the light of day. She would publish stories elsewhere and work on other novels, but she wouldn't return to the blue-bear manuscript for another ten years.

Monona Wali's *My Blue Skin Lover*

Monona Wali grew up learning about the twelfth-century mystical poet Akka Mahadevi from her father. The story is that Akka Mahadevi rejected wealth, privilege, and marriage in favor of enlightenment and her love of the god Shiva. Mahadevi's collected poetry records these decisions and choices. Ultimately, Mahadevi is considered by many scholars to be an important early figure in the movement for women's equality and emancipation.

Monona had mostly forgotten those stories as she grew into an adult and became a successful documentary filmmaker. Her documentary *María's Story* follows María Serrano, a Salvadoran guerrilla leader during the 1989 conflicts there. It won numerous honors and awards.

Monona later turned to writing, finishing an unpublished manuscript that she now considers to have been necessary practice. When she shelved that project and looked for another to jump into, she and her father again discussed the poet Akka Mahadevi. Her father asked her if she'd consider making a film about Mahadevi.

So Monona wrote a treatment for a screenplay, set in the twelfth century, but she didn't go further because it didn't feel right. Years later Monona was inspired to modernize the story. "It came to me sort of in a flash. What would it look like if somebody took the god Shiva as their lover in contemporary America?"

That question drove her, and as she thought about it, she realized she needed to write a novel rather than make a film. She had to create a character who—like the girl in the poems—would abandon her marriage, her family, and all life's comforts. Monona could show that inner journey much more easily via a novel, and so she started writing.

The contemporary setting allowed Monona to drop some elements of Akka Mahadevi's poems, while adding others that allowed her to explore place and culture in modern America. Monona admits it was a stretch for her at first because of its mystical, magical elements, but she couldn't resist the story. She finished the first draft within a matter of months.

But like her first, unpublished manuscript, *My Blue Skin Lover* seemed destined never to see the light of day. How it actually came to be published is a story for down the road.

Cynthia Bond's *Ruby*

For Cynthia Bond, *Ruby* began with a shirt. Cynthia was dealing with depression and some traumatic events in her life, so at the suggestion of a friend, she enrolled in a community education class to try to reconnect to her creative side. By the time the class began, she had started wearing the same gray shirt almost every day. It matched her inner mood, and she couldn't seem to find the interest to wear anything else. In the first class session the students worked on creating metaphors, and Cynthia wrote this sentence: "She wore gray like rain clouds."

It's pretty rare that a writer can trace back to the first sentence of an epic three-volume story, but that was the moment. Cynthia Bond was just trying to imagine a woman who wore the gray shirt. She had no idea how far that line would take her.

Though they had the shirt in common, the more Cynthia wrote about this woman, the more she realized it wasn't her. It was a character with different life experiences, and Cynthia became engrossed with the details of her character's life story. We now know the woman on those early journal pages as Ruby Bell from *Ruby*. She just "started showing up every time I went to that writing class," Cynthia recalls.

Later, as she continued to write, other characters started to join the fold, so many that before Cynthia had much of a story, she had notebooks full of characters and their individual histories. That's when she realized this wasn't just an exercise — she needed to take it seriously as a bigger story. Not only that, she knew this story was important. Because of her own challenging experiences and her ongoing social-service work with homeless youth in Los Angeles, Cynthia knew she needed to tell the story of *Ruby* and tell it well.

In the coming months and years, Cynthia would turn her attention to structuring a framework to tell these characters' stories. She would have to deal with a number of setbacks and delays, but the feeling that this set of stories needed to be told kept her committed to the process.

Zetta Elliott's *Bird*

Zetta Elliott began *Bird* with a lot on her mind. She says she always writes in phases and needs to focus on the element that is driving her at the time. She'd moved to Athens, Ohio, in 2001 for a dissertation fellowship, but her dissertation receded in her mind a few weeks later, after the September 11 terrorist attacks.

Zetta had grown up in New York, and having just moved to Ohio, she couldn't get the city of her childhood out of her mind. She missed it. She hurt for it. She wanted to be there for it. "To be away from New York when there was so much going on in the city was really difficult, and instead of focusing on my dissertation, which was about representations of racial violence and trauma, I just wrote a whole bunch of books for kids set in New York."

In the five days after the World Trade Center towers fell, Zetta wrote six children's picture-book manuscripts. One of those was *Bird*. Zetta says the story behind *Bird* had always been with her — it was the most personal of the stories she wrote. The attacks in New York only added to her sense of urgency in writing it.

Though the September 11 attacks prompted the urgency to write, the purpose behind *Bird* came from somewhere else entirely. Zetta had grown up watching the impact of addiction in the life of her older brother, and she had always wanted to write a story for kids that would help them talk about and share the experience of living through those circumstances.

Zetta knew there were thousands of children like her. Kids were growing up with family members who were unreliable, absent, incarcerated, in trouble, or in treatment, and they didn't have the language or life experience to be able to understand it or talk about it.

Stories of a family member's addiction aren't typical in children's picture books. But she felt that made *Bird* even more important to write: "Bookshelves don't need stories that are already there."

So she wrote the draft of *Bird* in the fallout of that dark period in American history. But years would pass before *Bird* found a publisher. Zetta would have to spend many years fighting to maintain her vision for *Bird* and to make sure the book missing from children's shelves could one day be found there.

Delilah Dawson's *Wicked as They Come*

Sometimes our best ideas come in our sleep. Dreams are a powerful tool of the subconscious, and when Delilah Dawson dreamed of a man in a forest, it started her down the path to creating a whole new world. At the time she had the dream, Delilah had already written an unsold book for children.

In her dream, she woke in the middle of a strange forest. It was dark and misty and lined with tangled trees. She remembers the quiet of the forest too. A man leaned against one of the trees; he was dressed like Spike, a vampire character from *Buffy the Vampire Slayer*, which Delilah had been binge watching at the time.

Some writers keep dream journals or try to mine their dreams for story ideas. But Delilah didn't have a process like that, and she wasn't looking for this as a potential world for her next writing project. But as she notes, some dreams disappear and some stick with you. "This one had that stickiness to it," she says.

Delilah's background as a visual artist played a strong role in this initial spark of story. After writing about the man in her dream, she focused on the world. Intrigued by the snarled birch trees and the strange forest images from her dream, she was eager to begin building this new world. Based on just a few glimpses, she began to imagine other locations in this world and found herself wanting to spend more and more time there: "This was a world I wanted to dwell in. I wanted to live in that strange world of his. So he was the hook, but I wanted to be in that world with him, not place him in our world."

Within the context of origin stories, it's interesting that her initial writing focus was character and then setting. A contrast is frequently drawn between "genre" and "literary" fiction writers: genre writers focus on plot, while literary writers focus on character. Delilah's *Wicked as They Come* would be labeled a genre work, but she began squarely with her characters, and then with setting, before she ever started to weave together the plot elements.

Though her idea began with the intriguing dream character, Delilah realized quickly that it couldn't be his story, and she needed to find the person whose story it would be. As she crafted that new main character, named Tish, Delilah began building a plot that would introduce Tish into the story's emerging world. Delilah still marvels at the success of a book series that would never have been written but for one strange dream.

Alan Heathcock's *Volt*

Alan Heathcock started his short story collection *Volt* with the idea of a town named Krafton drowned in injustice and grief. Alan had finished his MFA and published a couple of short stories; he felt that meant he was ready to graduate from short fiction to his first novel. He'd always seen himself as a novelist, so he jumped in and wrote about 250 pages.

Alan followed the conventional wisdom he'd heard from day one of his writing program: you write in order to discover the story. But after reading those 250 pages, he came to a rather stark realization that I'll explore in depth later in the book: his pages weren't adding up to anything.

He tried to write his way forward, but he remembers that it was "kind of like a tractor pull where the farther you get, the more weight that shifts forward. In other words, I knew I'd have to backtrack almost all the way to the beginning to start moving forward again."

His story failed as a novel. But Alan wasn't ready to scrap everything. The whole might not have worked, yet there were sections, passages, characters, and moments that he just couldn't let go of. "So I was confronted with the question of what do I do now? The crushing truth that came back to me was that I didn't know."

Ultimately, after time away from the work, the answer struck Alan. The form that he'd been trying to "graduate from" was where he should have been all along. As Alan explains it, short stories are single dramatic movements, while novels link together many different dramatic movements. Alan realized that his problem was the linking, not the stories themselves. "Trapped in this big mess were powerful dramatic movements that were getting lost, so I extracted each of them, let them stand on their own, and I thought, well, now I have something here."

It was a difficult decision. Alan had to let go of the idea of himself as a novelist, at least for a time, and focus on championing this collection of connected short stories.

Clara Bensen's *No Baggage*

If there's an outlier in this group of authors, it is likely Clara Bensen's memoir, *No Baggage*. No matter the origin, our other authors were looking for stories when they found them. Clara Bensen was looking for many things after a slow recovery from a mental health crisis, but book topics certainly weren't among them. Early in her memoir Clara tells us that a quotation from Rilke's *Book of Hours*, "Let everything happen to you. Beauty and terror," became her postrecovery mantra. It guided her to jump at a spontaneous trip halfway around the world without a single piece of luggage. Just a few months earlier she would never have taken such a trip.

She had no intention of writing about the experience of her travels. This held true even when she returned home. After returning, she focused on figuring out her still undefined relationship with her traveling companion, Jeff. Five months after their return they were discussing the trip, and Jeff said, "You know, it's kind of a good story. You should write it up and send it somewhere."

So Clara wrote an essay and cold-submitted it to *Salon,* an online magazine. As she recalls, the original essay focused entirely on the minimalism of the trip. She titled it "21 Days, One Green Dress." Clara worked with the staff at *Salon* to revise the essay and, with their help and with Jeff's permission, added the spontaneous romantic element of the adventure. *Salon* ran the piece a few days later, changing just a few details and adding a new title, "The Craziest OK Cupid Date Ever."[3]

She recalls that it published in the evening, and by the next morning everything had changed. The article struck a nerve with readers, and "it was suddenly like, holy shit," says Clara. "Inbox exploding, phone ringing early in the morning." She heard from distant friends, close family, and strangers she'd never met before. Then, when she was almost ready to take a break from the inquiries and correspondence, literary agents and film scouts started to reach out. They told her they thought there could be a more extended story, and suddenly Clara had a decision to make about something she'd never considered before: Did she even want to write a book?

Finding a Path from an Idea

Whether it was a writing prompt, a dream, anger, speculation, or something else entirely, in each of these cases the initial spark of a story proved to be important, but not everything. The spark kindles the writer through long hours of doubt and decisions, but it is just the first step in the process. With the possible exception of Clara Bensen, whose idea found her, what unites these debut authors isn't where the spark came from but how they responded to it. In every case, whether they got to work right away or waited years, the authors opened themselves up to their idea and couldn't let go of it. Some were further along than others in their writing career, some returned to their idea much later, but no matter when they started writing, they all started thinking beyond that initial idea. They may not have immediately known how to do it, but they were all looking for paths to convert their idea into a story.

In many ways, learning how to look for story is the first skill of a storyteller. Isn't that what an idea is, after all? It's a new framework, a new unanswered question, a new meaning, or a new point of view. It's something worth sharing, worth enduring hours of misfires and doubts. It's worth all the effort that accompanies the long process of writing a book.

Out of Ideas?

Out of ideas? Trying to find a great idea? Here are ten methods other well-established writers have used to find their paths.

Read Ten Books

At the keynote for the Twelfth Annual Library of Congress Book Festival, author Junot Díaz said that if you feel bereft of ideas, read ten books in a row. "If you read ten books back to back, I promise you, you'll have ideas. Haven't you ever had that where you read two or three books and you're like, I can do this better, or, I can do this just as badly? Ten books every time you're stumped."*

Ignore the Forgettable Ones

So often we lament that we came up with ideas in bed, in the shower, while driving, or any other place where we can't immediately write them down. But if you can't remember the idea later, maybe it wasn't worth writing in the first place. In a 2011 *Atlan-*

---

* Paula Beltrán and translator, "Junot Díaz Gives Advice to Young Writers at the 12th Annual Library of Congress National Book Festival," *Huffington Post*, September 28, 2012, http://www.huffingtonpost.com /paula-beltr/junot-diaz-gives-advice_b_1913789.html.

tic interview, Stephen King explained why he never writes ideas down. "All you do when you write ideas down is kind of immortalize something that should go away. If they're bad ideas, they go away on their own."[*]

Just Write Badly

Naomi Epel's classic book on writing and creativity, *Writers Dreaming: Twenty-Six Writers Talk about Their Dreams and the Creative Process*, is well worth reading cover to cover. But one of the most famous pieces of advice from that book came from poet Maya Angelou: "What I try to do is write. I may write for two weeks 'the cat sat on the mat, that is that, not a rat.' And it might be just the most boring and awful stuff. But I try. When I'm writing, I write. And then it's as if the muse is convinced that I'm serious and says, 'Okay. Okay. I'll come.'"[†]

Look Again

In a 1984 *Paris Review* interview, James Baldwin revealed an important piece of wisdom that helped him throughout his writing career. One day when he was young, the painter Beauford Delaney was walking with him; he pointed to a puddle and asked Baldwin to look. "I looked and all I saw was water. And he said, 'Look again,' which I did, and I saw oil on the water and the city reflected in the puddle. It was a great revelation to me. I can't explain it. He taught me how to see, and how to trust what I saw."[‡]

Start with One True Sentence

In *A Moveable Feast*, Ernest Hemingway tells how he fought writer's block by challenging himself to narrow his focus to the smaller ele-

[*] James Parker, "Stephen King on the Creative Process, the State of Fiction, and More," *Atlantic*, April 12, 2011, http://www.theatlantic.com/entertainment/archive/2011/04/stephen-king-on-the-creative-process-the-state-of-fiction-and-more/237023/.

[†] Naomi Epel, *Writers Dreaming: Twenty-Six Writers Talk about Their Dreams and the Creative Process* (New York: Vintage, 1994).

[‡] Jordan Elgrably, "James Baldwin: The Art of Fiction No. 78," *Paris Review*, Spring 1984, http://www.theparisreview.org/interviews/2994/the-art-of-fiction-no-78-james-baldwin.

ments of his writing. Once he did that, he was off and running. He wrote that he would look out over the Paris rooftops and think, "Do not worry. You have always written before and you will write now. All you have to do is write one true sentence. Write the truest sentence that you know."*

Accept Imperfection

Anne Lamott in *Bird by Bird* talks about the powerful concept of shitty first drafts, and how the idea of perfection makes too many writers stumble. "Almost all good writing begins with terrible first efforts. You need to start somewhere."†

Make a Pie—or Something Else

Hilary Mantel wrote a 2010 article for the *Guardian* offering many pieces of advice for young writers. Among other things, she advised letting yourself do something else if you get stuck. "Take a walk, take a bath, go to sleep, make a pie, draw, listen to music, meditate, exercise; whatever you do, don't just stick there scowling at the problem."‡

Find the Butterfly

In a Loft *Writers' Block* interview with me, the poet Tracy K. Smith suggested following the advice of Yeats to seek that which is hopeful and alive. "A teacher once quoted Yeats in reminding me that the process of writing should be a joyful one: 'And wisdom is a butterfly / And not a gloomy bird of prey.' Even when we are exploring difficult material, there is a buoyancy that I try to remind myself to tap into — something hopeful and alive, and unflagging that can help carry me further into whatever it is that I'm pursuing."§

---

* Ernest Hemingway, *A Moveable Feast: The Restored Edition*, ed. Sean Hemingway (New York: Scribner, 2010).
† Anne Lamott, *Bird by Bird: Some Instructions on Writing and Life* (New York: Anchor Books, 1995).
‡ Hilary Mantel, "Hilary Mantel's Rules for Writers," *Guardian*, February 22, 2010, https://www.theguardian.com/books/2010/feb/22/hilary-mantel-rules-for-writers.
§ Tracy K. Smith, "Interview with Tracy K. Smith, Winner of 2012 Pulitzer Prize in Poetry," by Chris Jones *Writers' Block Blog, The Loft Literary Center*, April 17, 2012, https://writersblock.loft.org/2012/04/17/659/interview_with_tracy_k_smith_winner_of_2012_pulitzer_prize_in_poetry.

Just Dig Already

Cheryl Strayed in her book *Tiny Beautiful Things* challenges the struggling writer to stop wallowing and just get to work. "Writing is hard for every last one of us. . . . Coal mining is harder. Do you think miners stand around all day talking about how hard it is to mine for coal? They do not. They simply dig."[*]

Be Open to Inspiration

Finally, if you're still feeling stuck or just fascinated by the ideas behind the work, I highly recommend reading *Dancing with Mrs. Dalloway* by Celia Blue Johnson.[†] In this well-researched book you'll find the stories of inspiration behind fifty of the most beloved classics of all time. For instance, Jules Verne's *Around the World in Eighty Days* began because of a newspaper travel advertisement; *The Hobbit* began while J. R. R. Tolkien graded student papers and found a blank page in the stack; and Antoine de Saint-Exupéry wrote *The Little Prince* after surviving a plane crash in the Sahara.

[*] Cheryl Strayed, *Tiny Beautiful Things: Advice on Love and Life from Dear Sugar* (New York: Vintage, 2012).
[†] Celia Blue Johnson, *Dancing with Mrs. Dalloway: Stories of the Inspiration behind Great Works of Literature* (New York: Perigee Books, 2011).

2. Processing Process

Writers often ask each other about process. Go to any author reading with a Q&A, and after the "where do you get your ideas?" question, you'll quickly hear questions about process that range from the basic to the peculiar. What time of day do you write? Do you write every day? Do you ever write with a particular reader in mind? What scent of candle do you burn while writing? Are you always fully dressed?

It's not that the answers to this line of questioning aren't potentially interesting, but there's something we miss in asking them. The secrets and shortcuts of Great Writer X's process won't help another writer weave the same magic. Understanding how an author discovers their process and how they prepare to tackle narrative challenges is potentially far more instructive.

As an example, Eric Smith, author of *Inked*, developed an all-day Sunday writing practice. He protected his Sundays with vigor and sought to work as much as he could that day. He would supplement that work with one or two short periods during the week. That process has continued to work for him, but I don't think it is all that useful to learn that part of his process. The fact that Eric found a Sunday practice served him well doesn't mean much for us. How we sit (or stand), what time we start, or how we work does matter, but it varies dramatically writer to writer.

But what if instead of asking when he writes, we asked him how he approached those Sundays? How was his process effective, and did it allow him to keep to his commitment to get words on the page?

In my interviews, the most compelling process question came down to the old writing dilemma of plotter versus pantser. For these eleven authors, the decision to either plot out their book in advance or write it by the seat of their pants shaped almost all their other processes.

In this chapter we'll look at the *how* behind each author's approach to writing time, which can loosely be distilled into three methods: the planned approach, the organic approach, and the blended approach.

This is a decision that every writer needs to make for themselves, but we can learn from the approaches these authors took and the lessons they discovered along the way. Instead of trying to mirror their processes, we can compare their methods to our own and incorporate the parts that might improve our own. To facilitate that, this chapter explores the initial planning choices our authors made. But we'll also go beyond their initial steps and explore the other process-related patterns that emerged. We'll look at the other hows of process—the tricks, the experiences, and the confidences—that kept their work on track and convinced them to persevere and finish.

The Planned Approach

Many authors make writing without an outline sound like skydiving without a parachute. You may get to your goal pretty fast, but you definitely won't like the result. The authors who abide by the planned approach look at their work like a construction project, not wanting to lay any bricks until they know exactly what they're building.

While writing *The Borrower*, Rebecca Makkai learned that she needs to write with a plan. She played with the idea behind the book for many years, but it repeatedly stalled, in part because she hadn't developed her process yet. She had to cultivate that before she finally felt ready to write and finish the manuscript. "I would write little scenes from it; I would try to outline," she recalls. "I would fill up notebooks with brainstorming. Over those seven years, it was really a matter of poking away at it even as I worked much more diligently on my short stories."

After years of experimentation, when she fully dove into writing *The Borrower*, she discovered the great importance of outlining. For her, it didn't kill the process as some claim; it helped her shape it. "It doesn't mean taking all the joy out of it; it means developing more digestible versions of the same story so that you can see it as a whole."

She believes that part of the reason *The Borrower* took her so long to write was that she didn't take this approach from the beginning. She never felt sure where the narrative would end up, so every time she found herself stuck she had to go back and rewrite it from the beginning. It took ten years to finish a manuscript draft that she felt ready to shop to agents, and while she considers many of the fits, starts, and delays as part of her growth and development, she says they went beyond normal growing pains.

Rebecca doesn't want to repeat her experience with *The Borrower*. "I was having to undo and redo so much, and that's likely how I had to learn it, but I think if I was to write that book now, it would be a much more streamlined process."

The Borrower taught Rebecca a process of planning and outlining that she has used with her subsequent books. She says learning the outline approach may be especially important for writers who are transitioning from short stories to novels. With a short story, she argues, you can often write without a grand plan because you can see the whole—the beginning, middle, and end—without much outlining. A novel is a different beast, she says, and can't be changed or developed as easily on the fly.

Courtney Maum adhered to a strict outline for *I Am Having So*

Much Fun Here without You. At least that was true her second time around. Courtney's experience is unusual in that she resurrected a decade-old manuscript to work on it anew. When she pulled out that old manuscript, attempts to revise it just didn't work for her. She didn't feel connected to it. "I'm using words from someone who's ten years younger than I am now. The humor's not the same. The tonality's not the same. These aren't words I would use now."

She realized that the only way she could take on the project was to start completely from scratch using only the basic framework and the same characters. So she wrote out a plot outline from the original book and then discarded the original manuscript. Every word of it. But the plot outline from the original manuscript kept her on track as she rewrote the novel. "Even when I would veer away from it, I had this little cord that I was holding onto," Courtney says.

Even the most careful plan doesn't lead to a flawless process. Courtney's outline took several weeks to create, but she still had to change it again and again as she wrote. "I just had to keep blowing up different parts of the manuscript. Every time I started over, I created a new structured outline."

In her day jobs, Courtney had also worked in advertising and film, so by the time she reached her final published version of the manuscript, she had adopted the film-world practice of storyboarding to complement her outlines (for a look at the process of storyboarding, see the sidebar in chapter 5). This outlining and storyboarding process is now exclusively how she works on her writing, but it took many misfires and years to figure that out. "I definitely come from the egocentric school where I thought that I'd sit down and organically write a draft and that's the book. I thought I was that kind of writer for a long time, and I'm not."

Both Courtney and Rebecca have heard the argument that outlining creates calculated and stale stories, but neither of them buys it. Instead, having the plot figured out allows them to focus on the finer points of scenes and to tie in themes and character more coherently.

The outlining practice these authors carried forward from their debut books served them well in their subsequent projects. Courtney Maum took many months to write the outline for her second novel, *Touch*, but then she completed that book relatively quickly rather than leaving it in a box for ten years. And Rebecca Makkai's subsequent novel, *The Hundred-Year House*, is written backwards in time over one hundred years. Rebecca says the outlining lessons she learned from *The Borrower* made it possible for her to write such a complicated narrative.

The Organic Approach

The flip side of outlining is driven by a faith in discovery—faith that spontaneity will lead to more interesting paths than any planned route could ever devise. Monona Wali's *My Blue Skin Lover* was written almost entirely with that method.

"I'm a great believer in discovering the story as you go," says Monona. She points to Patricia Hampl as a strong influence on her work, and she follows Hampl's advice too. "She says you should write to find out what you know, and I really believe in that process."

Monona reports that she writes and writes, sometimes hundreds of pages, without ever plotting out or planning any aspect of the story. But the organic process will take Monona only so far. She says there's always a point when she reaches the "oh hell, how do I keep going now?" phase. "That's when I start to outline."

So though she calls herself an organic writer, there always comes a time when she needs to look at the format and structure of her story. She just thinks that moment needs to come much later in the writing process: not when you start but when you have the end in sight.

In a somewhat similar process, Edan Lepucki believes in the hundred-page outpour. She writes her first hundred pages without looking back—no self-editing, no doubt, no story plot or plan. She just plows through. Then she goes back, rereads, and starts to plot and revise based on those first hundred pages.

She admits that page 100 is arbitrary; it depends on the ultimate length of the book. But when she focuses on plot, structure, and pacing too early, she feels she's far too generous with herself. "You get to page 60 and you're like, all right, I'm on it, I've got it. It's very hard to see pacing issues at the opening of a novel."

In her experience, given the length of the novels she writes, page 100 is the approximate point at which the book gets much more complicated. By page 100 of *California*, her two main characters reach the Land, which is a major turning point for the story. "There is something instructive in writing until you reach that point. Then you can start asking more in-depth questions of your story: what are the problems, how can I fix them?"

She also says dealing with plot and structure at page 100 is much better than plowing through and finishing a flawed story. You'll have to fix those errors no matter what, but you can't see them early on, and you don't want to find them only when you've wrapped it up either. "It's much harder to face fixing three hundred pages than it is to face one hundred pages."

The Blended Approach

Most of our authors use a process that lands somewhere in the middle, blending planning and discovery. Delilah Dawson intentionally took that approach for *Wicked as They Come*. "I don't start writing until I know where it begins — the opening scene, the instigating factor that changes everything and sets the plot rolling — as well as the climax and the ending. That's the bare minimum."

In the case of *Wicked as They Come*, Delilah didn't start writing immediately after the dream that led her to a strange new world. First she needed to figure out the bones of the story, from the opening to the climactic scene when all seems lost for her characters. She worked out every major plot point in the story, but it was mostly in her head, and she did not construct anything that would resemble a traditional outline.

Then she started writing, and once she started, she didn't look back. With every book she's tackled, Delilah writes this way. Once she starts, she writes her first draft from front to back, start to finish, "no rereading, no self-editing, as fast and furious and dirty as possible. I think about it like carrying hot laundry from the dryer to the bed. You need to get it all there to decide what needs to be arranged, folded, or gathered. If you stop and pick up every stray sock, you're going to drop that whole damn load of laundry."

Brian Benson started his book at page 1, ready to write it straight through as well. Right after his long bike trip, he took his notebooks and his computer to a café and got started. You'll remember from the previous chapter that Brian wrote his first page and thought it was the best page ever written, only to return to it the next day and realize it was "garbage." So Brian tried to rewrite that page, and when he reread the rewrite the next day, it was bad. "So on the third day, I quit," he says.

Brian hadn't written anything like *Going Somewhere* before. He now understands that because he jumped in without any structure or plan, he quickly felt overwhelmed and lost. When he returned to the idea months later, he started in the middle of his story, thinking he'd write a short essay and leave it at that. That approach took the pressure of a book off his shoulders. This helped him get unstuck, but the short section wouldn't work as part of a larger narrative, and while writing it, he realized he still had a book-length story to tell. So he abandoned the short piece as well. Brian wonders whether he had to experience all that to come up with a final path for his book, but he wishes he had started with a rough outline. "I ended up trying to write to a logic that I established for a small part in the middle that didn't end up making sense for the whole book. Starting in the middle helped me get started, but it also meant I had to rework so much of what I wrote."

Like Brian, Alan Heathcock started out writing exclusively organically, but after two failed novels he had to retool his process in favor of a more blended approach. "One of the things I was taught was that 'real writers' just sit down and follow the character. Some people do that quite effectively, but I followed my characters into nothing for two whole novels."

Alan is a film buff. During graduate school he watched nearly a movie a day, in part because he liked it, but he was also trying to figure out how the great filmmakers told great stories. After studying movies from masters such as Hitchcock, Kurosawa, and Bergman, he started to see common approaches in their work, approaches he wanted to apply to his own work. So Alan ditched his organic writing process and began creating storyboards similar to what those filmmakers had used. In many ways, storyboarding is just another way to outline a story. He found that this helped every aspect of his story development and writing.

Alan felt sheepish about the practice. Part of him felt like he was cheating or copping out of the way "real" writers work. Most of his teachers and some of the writers he most admired disparaged outlining, and that was hard for Alan. "Cormac McCarthy, who is one of my writing heroes, said, 'Knowing where you're going is death.' That's the word he used, *death*. So it took me a while, but now I know complete spontaneity is not for me."

Beyond the Plan: Finding a Process That Endures

Process isn't just about outlines versus organic writing. It also encompasses the ways you connect passion to process, the ways you plug your personality and life experiences into your writing, and the ways you endure and ensure that you finish. Again, this can't be copied. It has to be found.

Zetta Elliott uses her lens as an educator to drive her writing. She's worked with youth for many years, and she knows there are important voices and stories that youth aren't able to find in existing books. She says she works best when she notices an absence in the book world, then strives to address it or change it. "I always have my educator hat on," she says. "When I sit down to write, I generally think about a classroom. And as someone who advocates for children of color, I generally look for who is missing out, and I advocate for the silences."

Edan Lepucki also uses her teaching background as a resource for her process. She teaches an intensive novel-writing class at Writing Workshops Los Angeles, which she helped found, and each time she teaches it, she feels she learns more about how manuscripts grow and evolve. "I've seen a lot of drafts from day one, seen how they've evolved. In some cases I've seen more than one of a student's novels, so I just feel like I've learned so much about novel writing while watching that process."

Alan Heathcock had to find a philosophy behind his writing process. He says "writing through character" or a point of empathy was always his most effective method. After he figured that out, he never let it go. "Once I took that as a kind of religious belief, then I had to develop a process that would get my imagination to a place where I could most effectively write that way."

A need for thoroughness pushed some authors to do research until they felt mentally ready to finish their writing. Research also was important for some of the authors to get them to a place where they could finish the work. Brian Benson, who was writing about a cross-country bike trip, decided he couldn't solely rely on his journal, so he quit his job and biked the trip backwards from Portland to Wisconsin as he revised the manuscript.

For Clara Bensen, research meant investigating the genre she wanted to write in. This was especially important to her because despite the viral success of her *Salon* article, she didn't want her book to be seen as just a summer beach read. The journey she writes about stemmed from intense personal struggles with mental health. She felt that if the book seemed too much like a romantic comedy, she'd be doing a disservice to herself and anyone else with mental health struggles. So she researched the memoir genre. *The Art of Time in Memoir* by Sven Birkerts provided the framework that she adapted. As we'll see in a later chapter, the influence of this craft book was huge in terms of her writing process.

Delilah Dawson uses music to find her writing zone. She creates book-specific playlists on Spotify before she begins writing. This approach is especially helpful for her when she works on multiple projects, sometimes in entirely different genres, and needs to move back and forth between them. The music keeps her head clear and associated with the right story. "The songs don't have to describe what's happening in the book, but it's more the feel of the book. And I behaviorally condition myself so that when I hear that music, I'm in the world of that book."

For Cynthia Bond, the hurdle was to find a way just to get through the content. Her subject matter was challenging, with painful echoes from her work with homeless youth and her own life experiences. So she reassured herself by ignoring the prospect of publication. "Each day, I had to tell myself that it would never be published because some of the things I was writing I had never wanted anyone to hear. Stories I'd heard, things I'd experienced—some of them were too horrible, so I kept telling myself that no one was ever going to read this."

Rebecca Makkai found the way forward with her novel by growing as a short story writer. She'd become a highly accomplished short-story writer before she started *The Borrower*, and while she gets discouraged when she sees young writers treat short stories like a vitamin they need to choke down before moving forward in their career, she acknowledges that "there's a tremendous amount to be said for writing short stories before you attempt to write a novel, because you can see arc and shape again and again before you try something so vast that you can't see the shape anymore."

But short stories didn't just help Rebecca with process; her success with that genre helped validate her pursuit of the novel. "My inclusion in *Best American Short Stories* came right after I had my first baby. If I had not had that, I would've had no idea that anyone would look at the novel, let alone publish it, so I don't know that I would have been able to say with any confidence, 'Hey honey, watch the baby for four hours while I write.'"

Confidence based on publication or awards can be an important part of the process, but inner confidence can also come from failure. Monona Wali finished a first novel that has not seen the light of day. But since Monona never had a formal education in writing, she chose to see her first book as her training ground. "When I started *My Blue Skin Lover*, I had this whole other level of confidence. The voice was so strong. I mean, I don't think you ever really know what you're getting into with a novel. You don't. It's just such a crazy thing to do. But I did have a certain kind of confidence that I gained from working so long and so hard on that first, unpublished book."

Finding Your Process

Process cannot be taught or copied; it can only be learned through experiment and discovery. It doesn't really matter if one writer recommends waking up at dawn when they feel the freshest, or if another says to write by hand first or build a thorough outline. Again, these aren't really the key issues.

There is one ingredient in the process that all eleven of our authors share. These authors may hate or love revision, they may meticulously plot with outlines, storyboards, and note-card webs, or they may write like a car without headlights, discovering a track and backtracking when they run off the main road. They may have devised tricks or inspirations that keep them going. But at some point all of them played around enough to discover these things about themselves: the actions, routines, and experiences that kept them coming back. They took the time to develop a process that worked so that when they approached their writing, they could more easily get the words down on the page.

Clara Bensen struggled with doubts and uncertainty. Of all the authors profiled here, she was the least experienced when she started *No Baggage*, and as she tried to work on the book, she felt like she was "untangling a ball of yarn with a cat continually swiping it back into a huge tangle."

Her agent, Stacy Testa of Writers House, recognized this pattern in her author, and she knew that Clara just needed to get something concrete down so she could work on it further. "Clara is a perfectionist by nature, so she kept getting caught up in refining the work on a very micro level, and it was preventing her from moving on." When Stacy works with debut writers, she sees this happen a lot, and she urges writers to learn to move forward. "When you're writing a whole book, you can find yourself heading in surprising directions, and, as a result, you often end up scrapping whole paragraphs or even chapters. So you can't be precious along the way—why spend hours perfecting a single sentence when you might end up cutting the entire chapter at the end of the day?"

Every writer profiled for this book talked about this part of their process. At some point you just have to develop a method for regularly getting words down. It's the most important question of process: how do you stay committed and productive? It's not because the specific answer matters; it's because each writer must discover their own answers in order to finish their work.

"There are infinite choices at any moment as a writer and in your book," explains Delilah Dawson. "The hardest part as a writer is that a thousand shiny new ideas are not worth one shitty finished first draft. You have to get those words on the page to have something to work with."

To a person, these debut writers found a way to do just that.

Experimenting with Process

Everyone has to discover their own process, but here are ideas from other authors for how to experiment and develop a method that works for you.

Let the Basics Arrange Themselves

Kurt Vonnegut wrote to his wife about his routine while he was away teaching in Iowa. In a letter republished in *Kurt Vonnegut: Letters*, he suggested that finding a schedule was perhaps important but it didn't make sense to plan out every detail, especially the basics. "In an unmoored life like mine, sleep and hunger and work arrange themselves to suit themselves, without consulting me. I'm just as glad they haven't consulted me about the tiresome details."[*]

Don't Fear the Dark

In his famous 1962 essay "The Creative Process," James Baldwin argues that the artist "must not take anything for granted" and must try to expose what the rest of society tries hard to ignore or cover up. If you aren't open to finding dark truths, to exploring things that couldn't or shouldn't be said, you might be leaving the important stuff out.[†]

Find the Stamina

In her 2002 book *Negotiating with the Dead: A Writer on Writing*, Margaret Atwood notes that most people at least give a passing thought to the notion that they could write a book one day. But she says it's not about considering a story you might like to tell; it's about finding a dedicated process and practice. Wanting to write is different from being a writer, and that's the best lesson for anyone who is developing their own writing process. "To put it in a more sinister way: everyone can dig a hole in a cemetery, but not everyone is a grave-digger. The latter takes a great deal more stamina and persistence."[‡]

"So Be It, See to It"

Octavia Butler was the first science-fiction writer to win a MacArthur Genius Grant. After her death in 2006, the Huntington Library inherited a number of her notebooks and materials. One notebook from 1988 shows just how important determination and self-confidence are to an aspiring writer. Among the passages handwritten on the back were the following: "I shall be a bestselling author . . . my books will be read by millions of people. I will buy a beautiful home in an excellent neighborhood. I will help poor black

[*] Kurt Vonnegut, *Kurt Vonnegut: Letters*, ed. Dan Wakefield (New York: Delacorte, 2012).
[†] James Baldwin, *The Price of the Ticket: Collected Nonfiction, 1948–1985* (New York: St. Martin's, 1985).
[‡] Margaret Atwood, *Negotiating with the Dead: A Writer on Writing* (New York: Anchor Books, 2003).

youngsters broaden their horizons. I will help poor black young-sters go to college. I will hire a car whenever I need to. My books will be read by millions of people. So be it, see to it!"[*]

Find Different Reasons to Write

Much of the wisdom out there is that writers need to discover their own process. That view is certainly consistent with the experience of our authors. But it's also worth noting that sometimes one writer might use different processes. In an interview about Cheryl Strayed's "Dear Sugar" persona, she said that most people have numerous reasons to write, and she encourages writers to try on as many different reasons as they can. "Writing forces you to locate your clarity."[†]

Find Your Stubborn Streak

In a 1996 interview with the Academy of Achievement, bestselling author Amy Tan said that having a stubborn streak had led to her growth as a writer. She argues that you need to take every idea, every piece of advice and test it through your own intelligence and process so that you know it is "equally important and meaningful to you."[‡]

Protect It

In 2010 the *Guardian* followed up on Elmore Leonard's famous essay "Ten Rules for Writing Fiction" by asking some leading authors to write their own list. What followed is truly worth a full read, but the most interesting thing was the number of similar ideas around protecting time, process, and work. Roddy Doyle advised to "restrict your browsing to a few websites a day." P. D.

[*] Kevin Durkin, "Celebrating Octavia Butler," *VERSO | The Huntington's Blog*, January 27, 2016, http://huntingtonblogs.org/2016/01/celebrating-octavia-butler/.

[†] Jenn Tardif, "Cheryl Strayed: On 'Binge Writing,' Doling Out Advice and Finding Clarity," *99U by Behance*, July 2, 2012, http://99u.com/articles/7190/cheryl-strayed-on-binge-writing-doling-out-advice-finding-clarity.

[‡] Amy Tan, "Amy Tan Interview—Academy of Achievement," *Achievement.org*, June 28, 1996, http://www.achievement.org/autodoc/page/tan0int-1.

James said, "Don't just plan to write — write." Andrew Motion advised, "Decide when in the day (or night) it best suits you to write, and organise your life accordingly." And finally, Zadie Smith wrote, "Protect the time and space in which you write. Keep everybody away from it, even the people who are most important to you."*

* Doyle and James from Diana Athill, Margaret Atwood, Roddy Doyle, Helen Dunmore, Geoff Dyer, Anne Enright, Richard Ford, Jonathan Franzen, Esther Freud, Neil Gaiman, David Hare, P. D. James, AL Kennedy, Elmore Leonard, "Ten Rules for Writing Fiction," pt. 1, *Guardian*, February 19, 2010, https://www.theguardian.com/books/2010/feb/20/ten-rules-for-writing-fiction-part-one.; Motion and Smith from Hilary Mantel, Michael Moorcock, Michael Morpurgo, Andrew Motion, Joyce Carol Oates, Annie Proulx, Philip Pullman, Ian Rankin, Will Self, Helen Simpson, Zadie Smith, Colm Tóibín, Rose Tremain, Sarah Waters, Jeanette Winterson, "Ten Rules for Writing Fiction (Part Two)," *Guardian*, February 19, 2010, https://www.theguardian.com/books/2010/feb/20/10-rules-for-writing-fiction-part-two.

3. Sources of Support

Writing has a mythology to it, an image of the author based in the allure of rugged individualism. The word *author* stems from the Latin *auctorem*, which literally means "one who causes to grow," and in our modern era, the "one" part of that definition tends to be highly emphasized.

Franz Kafka, in an oft-quoted letter replying to his fiancée's request to watch him while he wrote, said: "Listen, in that case I could not write at all. For writing means revealing oneself to excess. . . . That is why one can never be alone enough when one writes, why there can never be enough silence around one when one writes, why even night is not night enough."[1]

My reading of that statement is that when you're in the thick of writing, you need to protect yourself from distraction. Whatever Kafka meant, his sentiment is frequently interpreted as promoting the myth of the author as solo genius. The thinking extends into an assumption that great writers develop their craft through inspiration and perspiration, needing genius and time alone to produce masterful works.

But in my experience, and in our authors' experiences, reality rarely matches this myth. There's a big difference between someone peering over your shoulder while you work and a trusted set of eyes identifying the strengths and flaws of your manuscript draft.

It can be damaging for an aspiring author to buy into that solo myth too much. Most of our authors turned often to their networks to help get their first book out into the world. And those who struggled with finding a network longed for one and have developed it since their debut came out.

The Network

The influences of a support network can begin before a writer even decides to write. Many of the authors developed a love of writing and story through a lifetime of exposure to and experience with literature. Cynthia Bond's father was a professor at the University of Kansas, and as a child there, Cynthia met writers such as Gwendolyn Brooks, Sonia Sanchez, and Nikki Giovanni. Perhaps the greatest inspiration for her was meeting a debut author named Maya Angelou, whose book *I Know Why the Caged Bird Sings* had just been published. Maya Angelou even stayed with Cynthia's family, ate red beans and rice with them, and sang the blues at a party at their home that night. "I was so precocious, and I'm sure a little annoying," laughs Cynthia. "I just hopped up on her lap and said, 'Ms. Angelou, why *does* the caged bird sing?'"

Maya Angelou's response stuck with her. Angelou didn't give her a glib or dismissive answer; she took this nine-year-old's question very seriously and walked her through her thoughts on the book and why she wrote it. She told Cynthia that books have the power to tell stories that you can't just say out loud. "I'm always now remembering just how powerful that was for me as a little girl."

None of our other authors mentioned meeting famous writers as children, but like Cynthia, many grew up in households that valued language and writing. Rebecca Makkai, Monona Wali, and Zetta Elliott were all children of professors, which shaped their connection to writing and reading. Each of them remembers reading a lot and learning the structures of story from a young age.

But, of course, growing up in an academic household isn't essential. Early influences can come from a number of other corners. Delilah Dawson didn't grow up in an academic family, but she did grow up an avid reader and was "one of those girls who didn't want to be girly." So while she read a lot, she was dismissive of the whole genre of romance. She assumed it was littered with pink hearts and flowery language.

Before she ever tried to write *Wicked as They Come*, a good friend of Delilah's named Jan gave her *Outlander* by Diana Gabaldon. Delilah protested, mocking the flowers on the cover and telling her friend she refused to read trash. But Jan asked Delilah to trust her and insisted she read it. Delilah read the first chapter reluctantly, determined to quit the book at the first awkward phrase. But she didn't put it down until she finished it. She was hooked, and couldn't believe how wrong she'd been. As she read more books like *Outlander*, she was amazed at the scope and possibilities within a genre she'd dismissed whole cloth. It was "so much more than a bodice ripper," marvels Delilah. "It made me realize that romance without characters and a storyline is as bad as any book without characters and a storyline."

So Delilah dove into the genre, finding the romances that were well researched with richly developed and relatable characters. The clichés of the genre had kept her from even considering writing in it, but she realized she had been wrong. "I had assumed that's all romance was, just some blabber around a series of sexual interludes, and there are a few books like that, but most of them don't stay on the shelf very long because romance readers demand more. They're very savvy."

Jan died a few years later, and Delilah says she wouldn't have the career she now has if Jan had not pressed that book into her hands. By the time Delilah had the dream about the man in the woods, she was open to writing a romance. Stories can find a writer in a variety of ways, but the writer also has to be open to the idea of the story.

Similarly, Eric Smith was open to the idea of writing in a new genre. He was working in the publishing world at Quirk Books and was already writing a nonfiction book. As recounted in chapter 1, a conversation about tattoos turned his mind toward a young-adult fantasy world. Eric had needed that kind of conversation—someone to bounce ideas off and someone steeped in the world of tattoos—to both inspire and develop his book.

But it wasn't just in idea generation that the members of Eric's support network had significant roles to play. He turned to them to help keep his project moving forward through all the struggles and dead ends. "I'm fortunate enough to have a pretty awesome support network in Philly. I have a writing group that I meet with who share bits and pieces of critique and suggestions when working on new projects. They were definitely helpful when it came to shaping the story and making the dialogue feel real. That's all I really look for when I'm getting notes, and they always delivered."

The decisions around sharing work—when to do it, what you want out of it, and how to address the feedback—are some of the most important that face a debut writer. Find the right set of people, with eyes you can trust, and you land in a place like Eric's.

One of the truths about writing is that you can never quite get outside your own head. The brain can make cognitive leaps that aren't on the page, and so that second set of eyes becomes essential to helping you find the gaps, the leaps, the jolts, and the sloth.

At the same time, feedback isn't always a good thing. Writers need to know what they want from it and how to handle it, or they can become stymied by indecision.

"You do have to protect yourself," says Courtney Maum. "You have to know where your center of gravity is, and your level of comfort and confidence. You have to know when you can accept criticism. I've taken people's comments when I wasn't ready to hear them, and it adversely affected the thing I was working on." She's learned over time that she needs to be confident in her work before she seeks feedback from others. She can't seek feedback when she's stuck. "For me, it's dangerous having too many cooks in the kitchen before you even know what's on the menu."

Alan Heathcock found that some aspects of advice and feedback could lead him astray as well. He valued his MFA experience, but he always felt like he was getting feedback too early, before his stories had the time to breathe and develop in his own mind. So after he graduated from the program he developed a concept of containment, which he still practices. "I believe in containment. I hold on to the work as long as I think it needs to be there. I don't see much advantage to having people read my early drafts. Sometimes I'll have conversations with my wife to help me talk through an idea, but that's different from her reading it."

Most of our authors don't follow Alan's containment practice, and sometimes sharing too early led them astray. Monona Wali hired an editor to help her with her manuscript, and it took her down some wrong paths. This editor had helped numerous writers and had successfully edited some well-known books, so Monona just accepted his recommendations without question. "That's when I think I ran into trouble. Some of his notes were quite good and helpful, but overall the novel became something very different from what I originally intended."

Monona spent a lot of time ballooning her manuscript up to 350 pages from 200, based on the feedback from that editor. She added characters and scenes, and soon the story had lost its center. Then, as we'll see in a later chapter, she had to return to her original intention. She's still glad she hired the editor in some respects because his suggestions did help parts of her manuscript, but it took a lot of rewriting to get back to square one after she tried implementing other recommendations. Based on this experience, she asserts that you can't just accept edits, even those coming from a respected source, without carefully considering your project and purpose.

There can also be truly bad feedback, advice that a writer needs to disregard altogether. Edan Lepucki thinks identifying the different types of feedback was one of the best skills she developed during her MFA program at the Iowa Writers' Workshop. "You hear criticism that you know right away is the right thing to do—that you've just been denying to yourself all along because maybe it's too hard. Then there's the criticism where you know immediately, 'Well, that's not right for me.' And then there's that third kind where you don't know how you feel about it. It might make you uncomfortable, and you need to take some time to think it over and make a decision. That's usually the best kind."

So unlike Kafka's lone writer, most of the writers profiled for this book recognized the importance of feedback at some point in their process. When they did seek it out, whether they felt ready for it or not, they had to learn how to wade through it, trust their instincts, and either accommodate it or reject it.

Many honed those instincts with a mentor or teacher. Of the eleven authors profiled for this book, only Edan Lepucki and Alan Heathcock graduated from MFA programs, but whether or not our profiled writers earned a formal degree, mentoring was part of their growth process. Cynthia Bond, Eric Smith, Monona Wali, and Zetta Elliott all obtained non-MFA advanced degrees, and although this education wasn't directly focused on writing, they point to it as important to their work.

Cynthia credits the publishing professionals who helped her pull her final manuscript into shape, but before she got to that point, several professors, including Henry Kisor and Jim Pickett, helped develop her eye and her ability to write confidently. Perhaps most influential on her work was John Rechy, author of *City of Night*. "He was the best teacher. He was the one that helped me find the *important* detail. He said including every detail was like watching a great dancer do pirouette after pirouette after pirouette. They may be spectacular, but after a while you just get bored."

The most important lesson Cynthia carried from her academic mentors was to tell her best story. When she started out, she says, her primary interest was to find a way to teach the reader something. But her mentors asked a different set of questions about her work, and it changed how she approached her writing. "Ultimately, for all of these teachers, it came down to the question 'Does the story work?' They convinced me that you cannot write a story to convey some kind of educational message. The goal of a story is to follow these characters as they learn and understand and reach a spiritual, emotional, or physical crisis, and then they learn or gain something as a result. They are then changed forever, and oddly enough, if you do that and it is true, then the educational message is in the story."

Monona Wali also credits a mentor with helping get her manuscript out in the world. After her challenges with the editor she hired, Monona turned to a writing teacher at Santa Monica College named Jim Crusoe. He'd become a friend and had a reputation as a really great teacher. He read her manuscript and liked it, but also told her he felt the middle of the manuscript dragged without much happening. He told her she couldn't simply rely on a big beginning and ending, with a bunch of connecting scenes in the middle. The reader had to keep being drawn forward through each section of the story. "A light bulb kind of went off for me then. I understood that I had to keep raising the stakes in the story."

Monona turned her attention back to the middle part of the story and added several elements to keep the novel progressing. "All this stuff like the pregnancy, her going mad—all that entered in the later draft after this realization. I couldn't just keep plugging along, going along nicely. Bad things had to happen to her in order for the story to mean anything."

Beyond professors and degree programs, Brian Benson and Courtney Maum sought training through organizations that offered creative writing workshops. Courtney Maum took classes through Gotham Writers Workshop. She followed them up with what she calls "summer camp for writers" at Tin House and Bread Loaf. She attended both of those summer programs the year before her book was published. "I credit those programs with getting it to the point I needed it to be to actually go through the publishing experience."

Brian Benson's sister signed him up for a workshop at the Attic, a Portland writing organization. After the workshop, he decided to sign up for a year-long intensive program at the Attic known as the Atheneum. That year it was cotaught by Karen Karbo and Cheryl Strayed. Strayed's book *Wild* was just about to be published when Brian arrived in her class. "That was a big move: it was pushing myself to take myself seriously as a writer." Brian says the year with

Karen and Cheryl helped his work in ways he can't even fully comprehend, but the most important thing he learned from them was developing structure and staying accountable to his work.

The writers who did not seek any kind of formal training, Delilah Dawson and Clara Bensen, still recognize people who mentored them through the world of publishing. At first Clara was reluctant to get any level of feedback on her work. She had been launched into the process of writing a book without ever really intending to do so. "I've done the whole writing career backwards," Clara says ruefully. "Now that the book is out there, I'm starting to establish myself in the writing community."

But she was terrified of feedback at first. She started by letting her agent, Stacy Testa, look through her work. Stacy explained much of what Clara could expect through the writing and publishing process. As she continued to work, Clara began sharing the manuscript with Jeff, her partner, who was a major character in the story. She had to sit him down after the book was sold and explain to him that "if you're this perfect guy all the time, it'll be boring. So I'm going to need to tell the truth."

Jeff had said he'd accept whatever she wanted to write. When she started sharing the work with him, though, she wondered if he'd still feel that way. "He did. He never asked me to change a word."

Then Clara started to show it to others who were close to her, including her mom and sister. Their responses were nearly all positive. But when she was about two-thirds done with the manuscript, she felt like she needed outside perspective. A friend was in a local writing workshop led by Abe Louise Young in her hometown of Austin, Texas. Her friend connected Clara to Abe with a simple handwritten note: "Take good care of her."

"Clara had a beautiful story, and her manuscript was 90 percent written," reports Abe. "Most of my job as a writing coach and editor was holding out a steady arm as she stepped off the boat onto a new landmass and life of her own creation."

Abe focused primarily on helping Clara perfect her sentences, deepen her themes, and stay on task to meet her tight deadline.

Mark Twain once wrote, "The difference between the almost right word and the right word is really a large matter—'tis the difference between the lightning-bug and the lightning." Abe saw Clara's first task as going line by line through her manuscript and, as she put it, "underlining lightning and striking through lightning bugs."

But beyond tightening up the sentences, Abe helped Clara's strong empathetic streak shine through. She recognized Clara as culturally sensitive and "aware of colonial history, ethical issues in tourism, and the unique privileges of being a white American." But there were elements of the manuscript where that sensitivity felt muted. So Abe helped Clara identify sentences like "She didn't speak English, so we couldn't communicate," and revise them along the lines of "I didn't speak Hungarian, so we couldn't communicate."

But perhaps Abe helped Clara most by keeping her on deadline. When Clara reached out to Abe, she already was under a tight deadline of about three weeks, but they had to "shift into racehorse pace" when Clara got a call from her editor: she needed the manuscript early to get a galley ready for a national librarians' conference. They would basically have a week to refine and revise the entire manuscript. "She worked by day and I worked by night," explains Abe. "Clara sent her new writing around dusk; I got new edits back to her by dawn. In that compressed, intense time her book completely matured."

Like Clara, Delilah Dawson developed a team of readers to help her as she worked on *Wicked as They Come*, a paranormal romance. Those readers were immensely helpful as she wrote the dreaded sex scene. Scenes with sex can be bogged down in overblown language. "With a sex scene, you want to keep the reader in the scene so much that they don't even notice what you're saying. You don't want your reader wondering why you used a certain word, or saying 'eww' or 'gross.' I think having layers of readers can help in watching your vocabulary."

But before she turned to her agent and critique partners, Delilah shared her first sex scene with her husband. "He was the first person that I allowed to read it, and I said to him, 'If you laugh at me, I will walk out the door and leave you with the children for the rest of your life,' so he was heavily invested in not laughing."

She then cultivated some early readers among female neighbors that she knew read the genre. Whenever she gave pieces to them, she asked for specific feedback. "I don't get a lot out of beta readers when I say, 'What'd you think?' because they just say, 'I liked it.' But when I say, 'Did this character work for you?' or 'Did you find the sex scene hot?' or 'Were there any parts of the story that didn't seem to work?,' I'd get much more constructive feedback."

Zetta Elliott found asking specific questions works best for her too. She spends enough time with her work that she rarely looks for general feedback. In fact, she even balks at the idea of drafts. "I would say that in some ways I don't do drafts. I work until my work is done, and then I ask for specific feedback."

It's not that she thinks her work doesn't need to be polished or edited, but she reaches a point in her process where many aspects of her story are nonnegotiable. So when Zetta seeks feedback, she's looking for copy edits or a specific craft element that she might want to fine-tune.

Whatever type of feedback this group of writers sought, they turned to outside readers. But who they turned to was often a little surprising. Aspiring writers are often told to find a neutral outsider voice, someone who isn't going to butter you up with false flattery or be afraid to tell you the truth about a flat section.

Yet many of the writers profiled in this book found help through parents or partners. Cynthia Bond, Monona Wali, and Rebecca Makkai turned to their parents. Monona Wali's father was the one who had pointed her in the direction of Akka Mahadevi's poetry, which was the entire inspiration for *My Blue Skin Lover*. Rebecca Makkai didn't know many writers when she was starting out, which she says "would be a huge joke now. I'm so steeped in that world now." So she shared her writing with her mom as she worked on it. "I know no one ever says that," says Rebecca. "But she is a retired linguistics professor and ran an academic press. It's nearly impossible for a typo to get past her."

Spouses or partners also served as first readers for many of the writers. Rebecca Makkai, Edan Lepucki, Delilah Dawson, Clara Bensen, and Alan Heathcock all share their work first with their partner to get a sense of where they stand. Edan shares her early drafts with her husband, and she's not looking for an intensive critique at that point—she's mostly looking for her bearings. "He'll say something like 'Oh, I was thinking that was going to happen' or 'That took me by surprise.' Just something that will expand my idea of what is possible with the drama."

Rebecca eased into that type of critique relationship with her husband. When she first showed him her work, she had not developed very thick skin, and she'd "often end up in tears even though he'd been totally nice." Now they're in a much different place. "I've been torn apart on the front page of the *New York Times* arts section; there's not much he can say that's going to hurt my feelings anymore." So now she always shares her early work with him to get his sense of it.

She's come a long way, though—when Rebecca was working on *The Borrower*, she didn't even feel comfortable telling her husband that she was working on a novel. "For the longest time, I'd call it 'something longer.' I think he knew what I meant, but I just felt so insecure. It felt so pretentious to say 'novel' when I only had twenty pages of it."

The Sacrifices

Most of the writers profiled for this book had support networks beyond the people with whom they shared their early work. "I guess I'm really fortunate that I've always had support of family and friends with my writing," says Edan Lepucki. "There are many people with families who think they're stupid to be doing this kind of work."

This is a sentiment shared by most of our authors, and yet many had to make great sacrifices to get their first book out in the world. Sometimes those sacrifices landed on the most important people in their lives.

For some, those sacrifices meant adhering to tight deadlines that had little to do with publishing schedules. Interestingly, several of the authors profiled here were pregnant while they worked to publish their first book. Rebecca Makkai, Edan Lepucki, and Courtney Maum all found the deadline of having a baby driving their manuscript deadlines. They each knew they would be too busy and tired to write much in the early months of motherhood, so they committed themselves to finishing their manuscripts before they gave birth.

When Courtney's agent urged her to resuscitate her ten-year-old manuscript, she had just found out she was two months pregnant. It would have been easy to let that manuscript continue to languish — after all, she'd already tried it out and it had gone nowhere. But she thought, "*I've been given a second chance here, and if I'm going to take it, I have to take it now. I have no idea what motherhood's going to be like, and maybe I'll never write again.* So I rewrote it from scratch, revised it maybe nine times, and sold it, all before the baby was born."

For some the greatest pressures and sacrifices around their first book were financial. Brian Benson quit his job in the final stages of writing *Going Somewhere* and committed himself full time to writing it. It was a huge leap of faith in himself and in the project. During that time he not only finished the manuscript but, as noted earlier, biked back across the country along the same route.

Alan Heathcock needed time to get his stories ready for the *Volt* manuscript, so he cut back his teaching load at Boise State University. And that meant a smaller paycheck. "We sacrificed as a family so I could write," says Alan. "I have three kids, so it would always be negotiating that time, but most days I found some time to write. My wife believes in me completely, so she would encourage me to make sure I had enough time and that I was a writer first."

When it wasn't financial or deadline sacrifices, it was people helping our authors with the gift of time. Spouses, parents, and friends all found themselves pitching in while the writers wrote, taking on more than their share of tasks or childcare, and understanding that social or other gatherings weren't always possible. It's the kind of gift that is hard to repay.

Web of Support

Whether it was friends, neighbors, teachers, hired help, parents, or partners, supporters played a key role in each author's march toward first publication. Absent those support networks, most of our authors wouldn't have finished their books. And that's just accounting for the first circle of support; it glosses over the other texts and writers that these authors turned to or learned from as they developed their craft.

More often than not, a good, deeply interconnected network is necessary for writers, and it takes work to develop. For aspiring writers, especially introverted ones, it can feel unobtainable. Maybe that's why Kafka's "lone writer" piece gets shared so often. The lone and weary genius is an intriguing idea. If it reflects reality, then all a writer has to do is sit down and get to work.

Hard work and talent are still essential—after all, no one else is going to attack that blank page for you. But as these authors demonstrate, establishing and nourishing community and connection is a significant part of most writers' lives. "It's plain and simple," says Eric Smith. "Without the support, my book doesn't exist."

Finding Support

Writing is a lonely art. There are, of course, exceptions: collaborative projects, writing groups focused on production rather than critique, and the writing rooms in television and movies. But for most writers, the practice takes place alone or in the company of strangers.

Saying writers need a support network and actually building one yourself are two entirely different things. Many writers are also introverts, which makes words like *networking* send a shiver or two down the spine. As this chapter has shown, every writer is different and needs to forge a support network that fits them. Some of our authors sought feedback early in the process from trusted readers, while others guarded their work closely until they thought it was ready for specific and detailed critiques. Many of these authors shared their first work with spouses or parents, while others strongly advise against this practice. Some took to social media, some found it an unwieldy time-suck.

So how do you negotiate all this, and how do you even begin? The best advice is probably to try everything and see what fits. Here are some options based on my conversations with our authors.

Communicate with the People Closest to You

A surprising number of our authors shared their work first with their spouses and parents. Yet many writing gurus advise against this practice. A quick Google search of "finding beta readers" leads to a number of articles with guidance like Amanda Shofner's 2014 post on *The Write Life*: "As easy as it is to get them to help, best friends, significant others, and family members are the worst beta readers. They know and love you, so they're predisposed to loving whatever you write — no matter how good it is."[*]

There's a conflict in all of this. The people closest to us can be great *or* awful beta readers, and it doesn't just come down to their sensibilities and reading skills. It can work or not work for a number of reasons, and it's not an evaluation or judgment on the rest of the relationship. The most important step is to have an honest conversation first. Tell them about your needs and discuss whether you're capable of working together that way.

Don't Fear Theft

If you're thinking you need nondisclosure agreements and lawyers to be able to share or talk about your work, you're doing it wrong. Don't be afraid of "the competition." Some aspiring writers don't want to share their work for fear that someone will steal their idea. As pointed out in chapter 1, though, best-selling books are rarely driven exclusively by an idea; they're driven by persistence, great writing, a knack for timing, and some luck. After all, there were many stories about wizard schools before the first Harry Potter came out.

---

[*] Amanda Shofner, "The Ultimate Guide to Working with Beta Readers," *Write Life*, July 30, 2014, http://social.thewritelife.com/ultimate-guide-to-beta-readers/.

Don't be afraid to share your writing, because you're not the first person to have this idea. Yes, even your best most secret, brilliant idea. Mark Twain wrote in one of his autobiographical chapters in the *North American Review*: "There is no such thing as a new idea. It is impossible. We simply take a lot of old ideas and put them into a sort of mental kaleidoscope. We give them a turn and they make new and curious combinations. We keep on turning and making new combinations indefinitely; but they are the same old pieces of colored glass that have been in use through all the ages."[*]

Seek Out Book Lovers

Even if you aren't close to being ready to publish, try to put yourself in places where you might meet other readers and writers. These could be author events, writing conferences, an MFA program, a literary center, book festivals, or libraries and bookstores.

But don't go just with the intention of "building your network." That happens organically the more you participate and engage. You aren't looking to *use* these people; you're looking to connect and foster relationships with them.

Give First

If you want a critique partner, put yourself out there as someone willing to do it for someone else. If you're looking for a writing group, offer to start or host one. Many of the online writing-group sites such as Scribophile require that participants critique other work before getting their own worked critiqued. The same philosophy holds true in real life, perhaps even more so. If it's all about you, you don't understand this whole community thing yet.

Get Social

In person is great, but not always possible, so cultivate those connections online too. Seek out a balance between the method you feel most comfortable with and the one that allows you to make

---

[*] Mark Twain, *The Complete Essays of Mark Twain*, ed. Charles Neider (New York: Da Capo, 2000).

the most worthwhile connections. Many writers prefer Twitter for this reason.

If you're already an active user of a social network, all the better. But if you aren't, take it slow. Get acclimated, actively observe how others, especially other writers, are using the platform, and try to follow suit. Nothing is worse than coming off like a used-car salesman on a network you've just joined.

As mentioned above, there are also online critique sites including Scribophile, Critters.org, and Critique Circle, among many others. It may work for you and it may not, but it's worth a try.

Finally, there are lots of great articles out there on developing your social media presence and connections. Read those, but here's one last tip: it's called social media for a reason. It's a lot like going to a giant cocktail party where you only know a few people. If you show up to that party with a neon sign flashing "I have a book" and a bullhorn so you can shout "Buy my book," people are going to start avoiding you pretty quickly. If, on the other hand, you act like a human being, start conversations, listen and respond, and help others out, you're going to have a lot more luck.

Toughen Up

Criticism, advice, and input can be hard to hear if you aren't ready and willing. It's a big deal both to listen to and to give criticism. You may even hear from critique partners who don't like or get your book. This is often the most useful kind of critique—so listen rather than try to explain. It's far better to hear about a confusing section from one person than from a chorus of readers and reviewers after publication. So be as gracious and kind as possible when giving or getting feedback. Even if you wildly disagree or the critique tears apart your favorite content, it's important to toughen up, listen, and consider it. It's a rare gift to receive feedback, and no one wants to keep giving that gift to someone who bristles or sulks every time it's given. Toughen up, then, be kind, and at least consider what you're hearing.

4. Craft Quandaries

In the photo puzzle game called Spot the Difference, children are challenged to comb through similar photos and identify the differences. The more particular and small the variations, the harder and more interesting the game becomes. The stories crafted by our eleven authors would not make for a particularly interesting game.

With tales of apocalypse, cross-country bike trips, magical fated tattoos, addiction through a child's eyes, small-town tragedy, unencumbered travel, love with a god, infidelity, kidnapping, sexual abuse, and an alternative world ruled by vampires, these books vary widely in subject matter and genre. But perhaps surprisingly, the craft challenges these authors faced had some striking commonalities.

Each story had its own problems to be solved, with craft elements unique to each, and I'll cover some of those toward the end of this chapter. But almost across the board, each author needed to grapple with two major areas of craft to complete their book: character and story.

The questions of character—whether a vampire or the self in a memoir—revolved around perspective, authenticity, and purpose. As each of the authors knew from the start, or learned as they worked, the actions and thoughts of their characters were the most important features of the book for readers. As we'll see, the writers had to let go of concerns about whether their characters were likable, about teaching the right lessons, or about conveying important plot points. First and foremost, the authors needed to focus on whether their characters were authentic and believable.

Of equal importance, the authors grappled with big craft questions around plot and story. For some, those questions drove their initial approach to their project. Others, through tough lessons learned, arrived at those questions much later. But they all came to realize how challenging it was to weave together the events and chronology depicted in their books. Most developed interesting methods for charting out those elements on the page.

If character and plot were the most commonly shared craft concerns, a secondary craft element came up again and again in my conversations with these writers: tone and format. They may not have all summarized it that way, but they all mentioned wrestling with cliché, expectations, and how much detail to include. As we'll see, these decisions, made throughout the process, shaped their work and helped produce the ultimate success of very disparate stories.

Creating Character

For many of our writers, character was where their story began. The authors wrestled with their characters' inner lives—their thoughts, opinions, and decisions—and their outer lives: their actions, inactions, and moments of dialogue. And at some point, most grappled with questions of perspective or point of view.

Rebecca Makkai channeled her outrage at the "pray the gay away" programs into a focus on how to tell that story most effectively. She knew the story had to be about a child in this situation, but as she considered her options, she felt that telling it from a child's perspective would not work well. "I just felt it would be manipulative or cutesy. Ultimately, it began forming in my mind around this person who wants to help but has no right to help. But who, unlike most people, would actually cross the line."

Rebecca needed to find that character in order to tell the story she wanted to tell. She continued to picture the child, and as mentioned earlier, she came up with an image of him hiding behind a plant. It took her several months to figure out the next steps, but that image stayed with her. Because she worked in a school, she started thinking of places where plants would be and began noticing them all around her. One day she went into the school library, where she saw plants at the end of the stacks. That was it — in a moment, all the disparate elements of character she'd been pondering for months came together: her main character would be a school librarian who would find a child hiding behind the library plants. And she would care enough about this child and his peers to get caught up in their lives a little too much. Rebecca started imagining the life of this small-town school librarian, and her story started coming together.

Delilah Dawson needed to find her main character too. She initially started to write about the man in a forest she'd dreamed about, treating him as the protagonist of her story, but although he felt like a fun, unusual hero to her, something seemed off. She realized that she was intrigued by the world of her dream largely because of her outsider's perspective, so she knew her main character needed to share that perspective. The man would be an inhabitant of the strange world, but he would be the love interest, not the hero. It wasn't until Delilah had devised a life and plan for her main character, Tish, that she felt comfortable moving forward with the book and both characters. "So I had to craft a heroine out of mud, and try to figure out who was the person who would most challenge and complement [the man I'd dreamed about]."

Now, many books later, Delilah has changed how she approaches creating character. She has come to recognize that conflict, whether interior or exterior, is the most important tool to establish character. "I'm still really proud of that first book, but Tish is given a pretty good deal in it. If I wrote this book now, I would torture her so much more."

For Edan Lepucki, the point-of-view question wasn't really that difficult. The book that she couldn't sell, the one she wrote before

California, was written in first person. She says that it was a retrospective voice looking back at herself as a teenager, "so it was like a thorny mess of bees stinging you all the time."

When she started *California*, she started writing in a close third-person voice and felt liberated by it. In some ways it was a reaction to the first manuscript and reflected her desire to avoid such an intimate voice; but further, the story of *California* just lent itself to the more distanced voice. In particular, the close third person felt important to Edan because she was shifting perspectives between the husband and the wife. "For me, point of view and whether it's first or third, or whatever, just seems to happen automatically. I have very rarely decided midway through that the point of view was wrong."

Finding Authenticity

Perspective and point of view are important questions, but once they've been resolved, the hard work of crafting authentic characters comes in. Almost every writer I interviewed for this book described efforts to fight against flat characters.

Clara Bensen realized that if her memoir was going to be more than just a longer version of her *Salon* article, she needed to develop the more personal side of herself on the page. In fact, she saw that side of herself—the part that struggled with a mental health crisis before going on the baggageless trip across the world—as the most important part of the story. She wanted to open up and tell the story of her crisis, in order to encourage more conversation around a topic that is often swept under the rug.

Once she made that decision, it was just a matter of finding the space and confidence to write about it and then sticking to it when it came down to revisions. "There were a few scenes that I was a little hesitant about, but for the most part, I actually fought for that more vulnerable and personal stuff. I wanted this book to have more depth and variety."

Brian Benson's memoir needed a similar sense of character. Brian read Vivian Gornick's *The Situation and the Story* as he worked on the book, and he credits her work with helping him find his own character. When he started to write, he didn't think of himself as a character on the page. Gornick urges writers of creative nonfiction to differentiate the "situation," or the events recounted in the narrative, from the "story," the things that underpin those events.[1] "So I figured out that the situation was the bike trip, but the story was my inner conflict over what lies ahead and what is immediately before me."

Brian admits that before he picked up Gornick's book, he'd mostly been writing about the situation—the events of his bike journey—not his internal story. So he needed to dive in and explore the personal story. That presented a new set of challenges. He notes that it's possible to identify the difference between those two elements and then consciously try to develop them both, "but figuring out how to intertwine those elements gracefully was the hardest part of writing the book."

Our fiction authors had to find ways to shape authentic characters as well. When Courtney Maum returned to her manuscript years after setting it aside, she began to realize why it had failed. It's worth noting that she hadn't exposed the earlier manuscript to outside critique, and she hadn't faced much criticism or rejection of her other writing. "I think I was writing in a very haughty or egocentric way. So when I finally picked it up ten years later, I was cringing. There was no empathy whatsoever; it was a vacant voice that I had written."

Over ten years of living her life, facing rejection, and reading works that she admired, Courtney says she realized that every character has to be authentic. That meant a cheating husband had to have moments when the reader could find his humanity and empathize with him. She says there is a huge difference between an unlikable narrator and an unreadable one. "I don't think the unlikable narrator actually exists. I think it's the poorly written unlikable narrator that exists. Look at *American Psycho*—that's an unlikable character, but it's compulsively readable. And what compulsively readable means to me is that in some way I can relate to the character."

Courtney had a lot of work to do to rewrite her entire manuscript, but once she recognized the lack of empathy in her first draft, she knew her chief task was to find the most relatable aspects of her "unlikable" main character. One key was identifying his emotional needs, such as his desire to piece his family back together. Whether he deserved that or not, identifying with it and putting it more clearly on the page helps the reader identify with his character.

Rebecca Makkai believes this authenticity is the most important task a writer takes on. "I'm always telling students that if you're going to write a seven-year-old girl and you don't know any seven-year-olds, you'd damn well better go babysit your friend's seven-year-old, because you don't remember what it was like. You were seven once, but that doesn't mean you know what it's like to talk like a seven-year-old anymore."

One of Rebecca's main characters, Ian, is a child, but she had lots to draw on when creating him. She says she was careful not to base Ian on any one boy she knew, but being an elementary school teacher helped her develop Ian's voice and perspective. "If you spend time around a certain age group, you get an ear for it. You have a great sense for what they know, what they don't know, and the vocabulary that's available to them."

The flip side of Rebecca's process was developing characters she didn't have a lot of experience with. *The Borrower* includes Russian immigrant characters, and though she knows a number of Hungarian immigrants, she doesn't know any Russians. "It would be a disservice to treat them like Hungarians," she notes. "You don't want to just give them a random butchering of English. If a Russian is going to butcher English, they'll do it in a very specific way. So I spent a lot of time on YouTube watching Russians do interviews and taking notes about speech patterns, looking for things like, what words do they leave out if they leave them out?"

For Zetta Elliott, keeping her characters authentic was everything, and she had to push back against a publisher request to change the age of her main character and the age group her story was written for. I'll examine her decision to stick to her guns in the revision chapter, but the lesson here is that sometimes deciding whether to say no is its own crafting quandary.

As Monona Wali worked on character, she heard from others that her main character, Anjali, needed more balance and depth. But Monona approached this problem in an interesting way: she added more secondary characters. "The thing about secondary characters is that I can have fun with them. You only have limited space for them, so you do have to create character sketches, and while trying to give them three dimensionality, they can also be kind of fun."

But the real point for Monona wasn't to have fun. In what might seem like a contradictory impulse, Monona created her secondary characters in order to advance and develop Anjali. The new characters and situations served to further define Anjali for the reader. For example, Anjali's sister became quite rebellious, not wanting anything to do with traditional Indian life. This change allowed Monona to show the pressures and inner crisis for Anjali between being "a dutiful daughter" and living the life she wanted to lead. Meanwhile Anjali's academic adviser become more rigid, pressuring Anjali to focus exclusively on the scientific method, statistics, and evidence. This change helped clarify Anjali's increasing desire to pursue something other than science. "So he represents a certain kind of knowledge. And ultimately, we realize that Anjali is seeking a different kind of knowledge."

These secondary characters helped Monona find a firmer footing for Anjali. She introduced people into Anjali's life who created pressures, questions, and conflicts, and once they were present, beta readers told her that her main character felt more complicated and authentic.

Keeping the Pages Turning

Whether an author starts with a character or a story idea, success depends on whether readers want to keep turning the page. This means writers need to diligently stay aware of why people read in the first place. The reasons may be different for each book or genre, but many of our authors said tracking those reasons and sticking to them was core to their process.

Although Delilah Dawson was writing in the romance genre, she initially struggled to write sex scenes. But ultimately she realized it was a clear expectation of the genre, and something that keeps people reading. "The first draft of *Wicked as They Come* was all blackout scenes: 'They had a sensual kiss, and the door slid shut.' And my agent and beta readers were like, 'Ummm, yeah, you're going to have to open that door.'"

Delilah described this experience on Chuck Wendig's *Terrible Minds* blog in a popular article titled "25 Humpalicious Steps to Writing Your First Sex Scene."[2] She wrote that post because she had struggled mightily with it herself and knows it's a difficult task for many writers. Also, sex scenes are frequently mocked. *Literary Review* in London has put on a Bad Sex in Fiction competition annually since 1993. According to the rules, "The purpose of the prize is to draw attention to poorly written, perfunctory or redundant passages of sexual description in modern fiction, and to discourage them." Every year the Bad Sex issue is the most popular issue of the review.

It's a hilarious award, but it's interesting that no other kind of scene in novels (violence, descriptive landscape, interior monologue . . .) is subject to celebrated mockery awards like this. Is it any wonder that writers like Delilah develop anxiety when they try to write about sex? But she had to get past that and move forward. "The key for me in all of this was losing inhibitions and self-judgment. I was so shy about it and so prudish because of the way I was raised, but I had to do it for the book and for the reader. It felt like to describe a sex scene was telling the world what I personally liked, but you aren't your book, you aren't your sex scene."

Delilah had to learn more than getting past story inhibitions. She also had to understand that to keep a reader turning the page, each scene needed a purpose. For example, the original manuscript of *Wicked as They Come* had the two main characters visiting a robot city. She said she initially wrote the scene because it sounded like fun. But it turned out that fun wasn't good enough. "This is the book that taught me that if you have a scene and someone says, 'This isn't working,' you have to look at it and instead of telling them why it *is* working, you have to make it matter. You have to tie that scene into the rest of the book and make it so that it can't possibly be removed. If you make everything matter from the start, you'll have a better answer to 'Well, why did they go to robot city?' 'Just for fun' is never enough."

But these kinds of plot considerations are only for genre fiction, right? Alan Heathcock says it was exactly this incorrect assumption that led him astray for many years. He doesn't remember a single conversation or class devoted to plot during his MFA program. "Plot was kind of the big no-no," says Alan. "Commercial novels interested themselves in plot, and we, as literary writers, interest ourselves in character and revelation."

Alan learned his lesson in the wake of his first two ill-fated novels. He spent several years working on them, but in the end he learned something powerful from their failure. "The education I got through these failed novels was that I didn't have a plot, and because I tried to write solely through revelation and character, I'd written my way into a whole mess of nothing."

Alan's short story collection *Volt* would rise out of those two unpublished novels. He took the best parts of each and constructed a collection of connected stories. Character and revelation were still key elements, but this time Alan added plot moments that he could map out and link together. "I could have my cake and eat it too. So the great educational point is that I can be deeply invested in plot without it becoming formulaic. And now I'm writing a long epic novel, and I'm deeply, deeply invested in plot. I think about plot probably more than anything else."

Alan's strategy for *Volt* and its plot revolved around what he calls "swivel moments." The most powerful aspects of his failed novels, the sections he couldn't let go of, involved intense moments of tragedy and injustice. Alan created those moments so he could explore their ripple effects. After he realized he needed to focus more on plot, he outlined how the swivel moments related to each other so he could tie them all together.

But Alan did something unusual. In his storyboard outline he emphasized certain moments that he knew his manuscript would *not* emphasize. They were significant plot points, but in his writing Alan was more interested in their aftermath and how they affected people's lives. "The tendency is to think that these are big huge moments, ripe for melodrama. That if you don't write them heavy, the reader won't understand that this is a big moment. But the truth is that we recognize its power if we just make it a true empathetic moment."

Plus, Alan argues, these moments are rarely melodramatic in real life. Often major turning points come quickly and quietly. "In my own life, these hugely dramatic moments—moments of profound injustice, or death, or tragedy—just happen. So it's my job to deliver the reader into these moments in just that way. And they *are* big moments—they're what I call the volt moments, from which I divined the title for the book—but the moment itself is not melodramatic. Frankly, part of the tragedy and the grief is the memory, and thinking that the moment should have been bigger but the world just continues on. This volt moment happens, and people are still going to grocery stores and watching football games and having fun conversations."

So Alan charted his plot points and wove them together, but though they were bullet points in his outline, he didn't overdescribe or linger on moments like a combine accident involving a child. His story was always more about how those moments intertwined and reflected off each other, but he couldn't access those parts of the story without making sure he was on solid footing.

Other Elements of Craft

In my interviews, all of our authors emphasized plot and character when they were discussing craft. But other significant elements came up frequently too, depending on the genre: backstory, humor, observation, and structure. This set of craft issues could be called *tone and format*—essential components for propelling and deepening stories.

For Eric Smith's *Inked*, restructuring became essential when he realized he had to make the world of the book more engrossing from page one. The reader needed to care more about the events of the story, and Eric decided that meant major revisions—cutting introductory and world-building elements that he'd originally created to ground the reader. By reworking his beginning and cutting some of the setting description, Eric was able to place the reader more immediately in the narrative, eager to learn what happens next. (For details of his process, see the revisions chapter.)

Inked is a book about magical tattoos, with an end-of-the-world urgency at its core, so restructuring to raise the stakes makes sense for that story. But surprisingly, the same issue came up for multiple types of book projects.

In *No Baggage*, Clara Bensen had trouble switching between chronologies—knowing when to place the reader in the now versus the then. The "now" sections were lighthearted, and the personal history section wasn't. "I really struggled at first in getting the tone right, switching between sections on this quarter-life crisis and then this romantic travel adventure. At first the flashback scenes were way too heavy-handed. They didn't go back and forth smoothly, so I had to really focus on fixing that."

As noted earlier, Clara turned to the craft book *The Art of Time in Memoir* by Sven Birkerts for guidance. Birkerts writes about the madeleine in *Remembrance of Things Past* and how eating that dessert as an adult conjures up all Proust's childhood memories associated with it.[3] Yet the moment is different; the experience of the madeleine can never be fully repeated as if Proust were again a child. This concept really resonated with Clara. She needed to find moments in her narrative where she could switch between the now of her journey and the past of her mental health struggles, and Birkerts helped her understand that she could achieve that through small, evocative details. She used those details to move in and out of past and present, improving the chronological structure of her narrative.

"Using small details to then expand was an important way of

thinking," explains Clara. "So *The Art of Time in Memoir* was important to my process, and I'm still learning how to narrow the focus and use a small detail to illuminate a bigger idea."

There are a number of examples in Clara's *No Baggage* narrative. In one section Clara weaves together news headlines about upheaval in Turkey, her parents' fears about her having been a "frightened hermit" just a few months earlier, and losing Jeff in the middle of a Turkish protest. In that moment she wonders whether her traveling companion has just abandoned her half a world from home. It's a striking moment, with rich details as varied as living off peanut butter sandwiches and a stranger with a Stetson hat that she follows during the turmoil, that allows Clara to weave together past, present, and fears for her future in a few short paragraphs.

A back-and-forth movement between then and now, backstory and urgency, also dominated Edan Lepucki's attention as she constructed *California*. Flashbacks are controversial, she acknowledges: people either love them or hate them. Edan equates them to time travel; to her, a sentence such as "Five years passed" "is the most amazing sentence. The fact that we can go backwards and forwards like that is such a gift we have as artists that I don't think we have in any other art form except film."

An essay titled "Braiding Time" by Cai Emmons in the book *Now Write!* has been one of Edan's big inspirations.[4] She challenged herself to use some of Emmons's ideas about flowing sentence to sentence between past, present, and future and combining it all into the same paragraph. Practicing this strategy helped her see "how you can literally braid time within even a single sentence. It is hard for flashbacks to feel integrated, and you want to avoid the foggy, misty feeling like you see in bad movies or TV shows when they go back into the past."

Beyond issues of chronology, our authors also had to consider the type of story they wanted to tell. For Zetta Elliott that meant learning the format that was appropriate for the ages she wanted to reach. When she first started sending her picture book manuscripts to publishers, they were 6,000–8,000 words long. An editor at Lee

& Low reached out to her and told Zetta that her work was interesting and distinctive but that most picture books for the age she was trying to reach were 1,500 words. So Zetta set out to study the form more closely and began to change the way she wrote. By the time she started writing *Bird*, she had mastered the form, so at that point it was just a matter of finding the story.

Monona Wali had to discover structure too as she switched from scripts to novel writing. But the visual aspect of film did influence her work on novels. "When you're writing a screenplay, it's really all about structure," says Monona. "It's about how you keep the story moving forward. You don't have the luxury of all the detailed descriptions or the poetry of language. So you start to see things in your head in a filmlike way, and that can help make something come alive on the page."

Monona took those screenwriting lessons to heart. Her first novel, which was never published, helped her learn the form and become comfortable with her voice. But it suffered from not having the same dedication to story that her screenwriting had. With *My Blue Skin Lover*, Monona considered the format of her work and the ways her scenes could be connected. She returned to some of her own scripts and others she admired, and applied those strategies to the novel. She focused on getting her ideas "to work within the framework of a compelling story that makes a reader want to turn the page."

Many of our authors report that they would go back through their work and find spots where the tone was off. As discussed earlier, for Monona Wali, developing secondary characters allowed her to explore her main character better. But those secondary characters also helped her shape some of the tonal elements throughout the novel, in particular the way her main character Anjali views family obligation or duty. Courtney Maum, too, changed the tone of her book in revision by enhancing the humorous elements. In reviews, *I Am Having So Much Fun Here without You* is often referred to as a black comedy, and Courtney says she did put effort into developing her narrative's humor. When she was revising it, she attended many live storytelling events and took note of the points when people laughed.

With some of those lessons, she went back through her entire manuscript to clean up and expand the humorous parts.

"What I was tending to do, I realized, was working way too hard. I would literally belabor a point. I think I doubted whether someone would think something was funny, so I would just push it so hard. Dry humor was certainly something I was not doing. It was very wet humor. So pulling back and trusting the reader to either get it or not get it was something I had to develop."

Dealing with Craft Up Front

When questioned about character, plot, structure, or other elements, many of these authors balked at the idea that there are craft quandaries common to all writers. Their sense was that working through craft issues was an individual process, and one that could even shift from project to project. But whether they were writing a memoir about a bike journey or an apocalyptic domestic drama, and whether they started with character or story as the backbone of their project, these authors ultimately had to wrestle with similar issues: character, plot, format, and tone.

The authors who didn't consider those elements early in the writing process expressed regret. Some had to address them much later through major revisions, while others had to abandon certain projects altogether because they hadn't considered these elements of craft.

Craft Resources

In the end, it all comes down to the manuscript. The idea, the support, the process, the publishing choices are all important, but craft carries the day.

This book was never intended to focus exclusively on craft, though, because there are already plenty of excellent resources available. More, in fact, than a single sidebar can do justice to. And the list below doesn't account for books on creativity and the writing life such as *Bird by Bird* by Anne Lamott, *If You Want to Write* by Brenda Ueland, and *Writing Down the Bones* by Natalie Goldberg. Others have been mentioned within the text. With those caveats, here are some great places to start if sharpening craft is your major aim.

Books on Craft

On Writing: A Memoir of the Craft by Stephen King | King, one of the most prolific writers of our time, provides one of the most in-depth and penetrating looks at the craft of writing. It's an extremely popular book for a reason.

Writing the Breakout Novel: Insider Advice for Taking Your Fiction to the Next Level by Donald Maass | Maass is a literary agent with an eye for what works in fiction. He has several books on craft, all of which are worth a read, but this is the one to start with. The book asks tough questions of your work and challenges you to think beyond simple revision, getting at the big picture of why you're writing in the first place.

The "Art of" Series from Graywolf Press | It's nearly impossible to pick just one title to recommend from this series written by some of the most well-regarded authors of our day. Each book covers a single important craft topic, including *The Art of Description* by Mark Doty, *The Art of Intimacy* by Stacey D'Erasmo, *The Art of Subtext* by Charles Baxter, and *The Art of Time in Memoir* by Sven Birkerts.

Story: Style, Structure, Substance, and the Principles of Screenwriting by Robert McKee | Screenwriting? Isn't this a book about *books*? Yes, but story is universal, and Robert McKee's classic book on screenwriting breaks down how some of the most successful movies rooted in the patterns that make all kinds of stories work. This isn't a rote formula guide for writing cliché and schlock; it's a reminder of why the stories that we all know so well actually work. More important, it can help you incorporate those elements into your own writing.

Wired for Story: The Writer's Guide to Using Brain Science to Hook Readers from the Very First Sentence by Lisa Cron | Still don't believe this story stuff is important? Lisa Cron's book investigates the brain science behind why some stories work and others don't. Cron argues that even the most perfect prose, the deftest metaphors, and the most complicated characters can still fall flat. Fortunately, her book suggests ways to rescue all of those features and make them work well.

Educational Resources

MFA programs are abundant in our day. Several of our authors earned MFAs to help them further their craft and career.

But most didn't. Many found other ways to learn their craft. Some sought help through local literary centers. Many cities have great literary organizations that offer classes on craft taught by renowned authors. I work for the Loft Literary Center in Minneapolis; other renowned centers include Hugo House in Seattle, Grub Street in Boston, Literary Arts and the Attic in Portland, Center for Fiction in New York, Lighthouse Writers in Denver, Writing Workshops Los Angeles in LA, the Writers' League of Texas in Austin, and the Writer's Center in Washington, DC. Do a quick internet search using the name of your city plus "literary center" or "writing classes" to find out if there's something near you. Even if nothing turns up, many of these institutions, as well as some national organizations, offer excellent online classes.

Finally, explore the many websites and magazines with thousands of articles on craft. There are far too many to list here, but venues such as *Poets and Writers, Writers Digest, Electric Lit, Millions,* and *Writer Unboxed* provide frequent craft-based articles.

5. Thorough Themes

Beyond their idea, their process, their craft, authors commonly face nagging doubts and questions about the depth and substance of what they're writing. Is this flat? Will this be meaningful to readers? Many reviewers and readers react to books primarily based on their broader themes. Themes make the story feel substantial, and ultimately gratifying to a reader. But how do writers create them, and are they intentional or accidental?

In 1946 William Wimsatt and Monroe Beardsley published an article titled "The Intentional Fallacy," which highlights the position of New School literary critics that "the design or intention of the author is neither available nor desirable as a standard for judging the success of a work of literary art."[1] In other words, the "intentional fallacy"—looking for intention behind an author's writing—is a fool's errand.

This idea was reinforced in 1967 when literary theorist Roland Barthes penned the essay "La mort de l'auteur" ("The Death of the Author"), in which he argues that not only does intention not matter, but neither does the author. Once words are written on the page, only those words matter. After that, the book is defined by its relationship to the reader or critic. No amount of context, no author statements about intentions, can outweigh the relationship between the reader and the text. And any themes or subtext that can be found in the work are entirely on the shoulders of the critic or reader, not the author.[2]

From these perspectives, it doesn't matter whether Edan Lepucki intended to include a strong underlying theme of truth versus secrets when she wrote *California*; this theme matters only if the critic or reader finds it in her book. In fact, in this school of criticism, knowing her intentions actually obscures the point. As Barthes wrote, "A text's unity lies not in its origins, but in its destination." So the origins (or authors) are not important; the destination (or readers) is.

From a critic's perspective, all this makes perfect sense. Critics need to evaluate only the product, not the process. But this vein of criticism has so dominated literary studies that many aspiring writers believe these ideas also apply to them *while they're writing.* That's not true. After an author publishes, their work is subject to such criticism. But most writers do bring thematic intentions to their work, and in this context it's worth considering them.

When asked to discuss the stronger themes in their books and how they developed, some of our authors claimed to avoid trying to find or follow themes, saying it hindered their process, while others employed meticulous methods to find, refine, and develop them. But regardless of their approach, and regardless of the validity of the intentional fallacy, it's safe to say that they all had intent while they wrote and revised.

Letting the Depth Emerge

Edan Lepucki is among the avoiders: she resisted thinking about the deeper thematic underpinnings in *California* as she wrote the book. It's similar to her approach to outlines, she says: "If I try it, it just kills any magic I have." Even as the story develops and those subjects start to emerge, Edan tries her best to "stay deaf to them."

She tries not to write out of order, which helps her control random urges to sprinkle thematic hints such as symbolism or metaphor across the text. "I feel very uncomfortable just adding random things and saying, 'Oh, I can take it out later.' I'm just too neurotic. I very much feel like I need to go through the drama in order to get at the emotional moment of the scene. So even if I know the deeper subject of a scene five chapters from now, I will force myself to write everything before then first just to be sure."

After she was deep into writing *California*, Edan did start to recognize some themes in it. Exploring secrets within a marriage is a major one. By putting a married couple in apocalyptic circumstances, Edan was able to expose and test the unspoken boundaries in an ordinary marriage. The genesis of her story was a secret object, the turkey baster, mentioned in chapter 1, but the theme of secrets seeped into much more than one object. Much of the conflict and tension between the characters has to do with knowledge—who it is shared with and who it is kept from—and there's always a larger sense that there are secrets beyond the characters that drive the functioning of their apocalyptic world.

But knowing all that didn't lead Edan to actively look for ways to use that theme throughout the book. "At about page 200 of the draft, there were some deeper subjects that I became aware of, and in some ways I tried to work toward them, but I didn't want to pay attention to them too much either. I knew that if I did, it would become too contrived or overly designed."

A few of our authors championed a more blended approach between conscious and subconscious development of themes. For *I Am Having So Much Fun Here without You*, Courtney Maum intended from the very beginning to use the painting of a blue bear as a grounding metaphor. The main character's painting depicts a stuffed blue bear seen through a keyhole of a door. He painted it while his wife was pregnant, and it follows its own journey in the book, reflecting Richard's shifting mindset around his marriage.

"With all the changes to my manuscript, the painting itself—what it depicted—never changed. A painting is so powerful, so much even more than a photograph, because someone's taken the time to do the brush strokes themselves. So it seemed a pretty obvious demonstration of the fact that Richard did have real love for his wife and family. It just seemed like a metaphor that people could relate to, whether or not they were married or whether or not they had a kid. I think the visual aids help you enter the story."

While the painting metaphor was intentional in her story, other elements were less planned out. In returning to her novel after many years, Courtney realized that one of the major failures of her earlier draft was that it didn't align the reader with her protagonist, Richard. He could be a cheat, but the reader had to feel some sense of hope for him; otherwise the second half of the book would fail. So while she didn't expect readers to approve of his choices, they did have to understand them and care where they led.

In order to do that, Courtney needed to create a beginning with thematic and tonal elements that "closed in on the reader," as she puts it. "I wanted to set up an atmosphere that was too close and claustrophobic and gray." Courtney could use elements like the painting of the blue bear to show that claustrophobia. As Richard's family life grows in tension and claustrophobia, he also begins to doubt his professional life. He now looks at a painting he once liked with a growing sense of disdain, and this shift can stand in for how he views everything in his own life. Through his eyes, the reader starts to see just how much his world is closing in on him, and comes to understand that Richard needs a change, even though the reader might not choose the change Richard chooses. In Courtney's first draft, she says, Richard seemed to cheat on his wife just for the sake of cheating. In her second draft, his choices are still his own, but readers can grasp the pressures that drive him to seek something different.

The exact same infidelity takes place in both drafts of the manuscript, but in the second one, because Courtney paid attention to the atmosphere of the early pages, Richard's needs and intentions are clearer. To achieve that feeling, Courtney had to not only show Richard's view of his world but also work against a strong literary trope, that of Paris as savior. "It was really important to me to announce to people that this is not going to be a book where the beauty of Paris will give you a new lease on life. This is the gritty version of Paris that I know and most Parisians know, that isn't perfect and always pretty, and that isn't going to give you a nice, clean exit strategy."

Courtney had some clear intention around the themes, tones, and metaphors for her book, and creating a world that would bring the reader closer to Richard's mindset. But there were other elements, particularly Richard's interactions with his wife, child, and business manager, that helped create that claustrophobic feeling, and many of those "were quite subconscious," says Courtney. "So it was deliberate to a certain extent, and then just subconscious to another."

Several of our other authors also came to their work fully intending to develop and build themes. But sometimes those intentions were led in other directions. Monona Wali wrote *My Blue Skin Lover* with the idea that the god Shiva would serve as a metaphor throughout her book. In early drafts, though, Shiva was always the hardest to write. And as she wrote, the story continued to feel flat. At the time Monona was in a master swim program and told her coach about the book she was writing. Her coach started asking her, "So this Shiva—how are you going to bring this guy into your book? Like in human form? I think the story needs that."

Monona resisted. It initially felt contrived, even ridiculous. "The idea that you would make a god a character in your story—I think it was a crazy idea."

But as she struggled with the manuscript, she considered that idea more and more. What if this thematic element, this metaphorical aspect of her character's inner journey, became a reality in her world? She decided to give it a try. "That idea helped me make it more of a story. When you put this god in your book, it changes things. For the longest time, I thought this book was about spiritual transformation—a book about a woman who gets enlightened. It took me a long time to realize it's more about a woman who's taking her life into her own hands and creating her own destiny. Shiva is just an ancient that allows that to happen, but not the end game. The end game is that she hopefully figures out the life she really wants to live."

Monona took another thematic risk by including selections of twelfth-century poetry throughout the book. They appear as passages the main character reads while certain events unfold. Monona admits that in many books, "if there's poetry, I just skip over it." But to establish the theme of transformation, she had to show how Anjali begins to see the world differently and read the poetry at a deeper level. Anjali "has to learn this stuff; it's not something she knows. She's discovering the poetry, the mythology; she's learning who Shiva is. As she learns, we the readers learn. So I hope that by keeping it really close to her, and her perspective, and what she's getting out of it, it became well integrated into the story."

Rebecca Makkai also had to let the themes develop in *The Borrower* as she wrote it. She started out knowing one thing with certainty: "My character was going to have to change internally pretty dramatically." From the very beginning, Rebecca used motifs from *Lolita*, *Huckleberry Finn*, and *The Wizard of Oz* as thematic markers throughout the book.

But even as she found a clearer direction for her character and some symbolic influences throughout, she knew from experience that themes become apparent through the act of writing. "Themes can't come out until you're a good way through the writing. They need to emerge. I think of writing fiction very much like I think of dreaming. We all write fiction as we're sleeping—we're telling ourselves stories, and meaning comes through in those stories in some way. At the point you start to tell a friend about it, you start to understand some deeper meaning. Those things will emerge in fiction if you just let them be. Some of them you're never aware of, but more often you start to pick up on the themes as you edit and reread and revise."

Planning to Find Themes

On the flip side, many writers profiled for this book used rigorous techniques to establish themes, symbols, and depth in their work. When Cynthia Bond started *Ruby*, before she decided to split what became a nine-hundred-plus-page manuscript into three linked novels, she had a lot to manage in terms of tracking themes and plot lines.

In her writing room, Cynthia had two pillars in front of her desk. She hung clotheslines between the pillars and plotted out the entire manuscript by attaching Post-its with clothespins "like handkerchiefs drying on a line." She used that to track and move scenes, plot elements, and symbols throughout the narrative. She says the visual cues from the clotheslines helped her most with the thematic elements of her book, in particular the haunting scenes with the Dybou. The Dybou is a spirit that consumes other spirits and represents hate and violence. It shows up in the narrative only rarely, but at crucial points. The figure stands in for much of Ruby's inner turmoil and the evils she has experienced and witnessed.

It was important to Cynthia that she not waste those moments, so they had to be carefully planned. She says she needed to be able to find those right moments in the original nine hundred pages. "I knew I needed to see it and be able to move those pieces around, so [tracking every scene with Post-its] helped a lot, and I couldn't have told this story without being very organized."

Planning was also important to Clara Bensen in writing her *No Baggage* memoir. As you may recall, when she set out to write it, she knew she didn't want a fluffy beach read. She wanted to go beyond the original article about her upbeat, spontaneous trip without baggage and explore the deeper issues behind that journey, including her struggles with mental health. But in order to do that, she had to carefully plan out the moments of flashback—where she focused on emotional struggles—versus the moments of narrative momentum. This was less a mission of structure and more to ensure that the elements of doubt, struggle, and recovery were present in the story without grinding the momentum to a halt.

So as Clara's draft took shape, she looked back at her original outline for the book and used it to track the major flashback scenes. This helped her identify the sections where she needed to pay the most attention.

She admits that her sudden fame and a quick deadline for her manuscript complicated some of these efforts. "Ideally in memoir, there's some space between what you're writing about. While writing this story, a lot of these themes were still unfolding in my real life," says Clara. With more time, she thinks she might have changed parts of the flashback scenes, and she might have preferred a more organic process rather than such a calculated one. But in the end, planning out where and how to insert those backstory elements allowed her to complete her manuscript by her deadline.

Two of our authors went even further in planning out the thematic aspects of their work. They both used an idea developed by Chuck Wendig in a blog post titled "25 Ways To Plot, Plan and Prep Your Story."[3] In revising *Going Somewhere*, Brian Benson developed a massive spreadsheet that included all the various themes he wanted to include throughout the book. "I tracked them chapter to chapter because I wanted to make sure in a really satisfying, mathematical way that all those different parts would come through."

One example of Brian's themes is the changing idea of Portland for the characters. It was the final destination of his bike trip, and over the course of the book, Portland comes to represent many different things: beginnings, endings, fantasy, reality, change, distance, hope, fear. It was very important to him that the idea of Portland shifted and changed as the story progressed. So Brian tracked it in a spreadsheet through the narrative "because otherwise it was too easy to get caught up and be too embedded in the moments. The being stuck in North Dakota, the being bored on the road, and not remembering to include anything about the past or where we were headed."

He says that after he started tracking the thematic elements this way, he began to see his manuscript differently. Not only did it help him develop the themes he most valued, but it also helped him fix parts of the narrative that weren't working well.

Delilah Dawson also used Wendig's spreadsheet strategy. Like Brian's, her tracking went beyond plot points. She made a sheet for each chapter, identifying the main plot points, the subtle plot points, the thematic elements, and the level of tension that each chapter developed. "If I had four chapters in a row with the same tension level,

I was doing something wrong. We need rising and falling moments of victory and conflict and pain and mercy instead of this flat 'Oh, they walked across this moat, and then they did this thing and saw a camel.' No, the camel has to spit at them and then they have to fall into a sinkhole."

Delilah says that after she first discovered this charting process, she read other authors' books and charted them out before employing charts for her own book. She remembers rereading Charlaine Harris's first Sookie Stackhouse book, *Dead until Dark*, and going through it piece by piece. She marked in the pages for the parts that drew her in the most, building a spreadsheet similar to what Wendig recommends. She realized that Harris's book kept complicating and intensifying the story, and she could see that unfold visually in the spreadsheet. This helped Delilah recognize why she wanted to keep reading the story and turning the pages. "I just didn't know it was possible to chart like that or why it worked. But you could start to see how this could work for any idea. Any idea could be a compelling story if you just do it well enough."

Alan Heathcock didn't use a spreadsheet to track his *Volt* narrative, but he did learn valuable lessons about building themes and plot into his work, and he learned them the hard way. As noted earlier, Alan initially tried to develop plot points as he wrote, but failing at this in two novels led him to realize he had to plan in advance.

So when it came time to turn those two failed novels into the linked stories that would become *Volt*, Alan had to find a process that worked for him. Turning to storyboarding, he mapped out the progression of the larger narrative. Because the short stories are linked, consistency was important, as was the direction each story took as it fit into the whole. "To me, story is a unit of communication," says Alan. "So the sooner I can get my head around precisely what I'm trying to say, the better off I'm going to be. Storyboarding is a very organic thing where I shift things in and out, but I find that it helps me to have my head around the whole."

This process also helped Alan decide the order for his stories. An author of a short story collection, especially linked stories, needs to carefully consider the order in which they'll be presented. He credits his editor at Graywolf, Fiona McCrae, for helping shape his thinking around the order. One of the first decisions they came to was starting the collection with a story called "Stained Freight."

Alan remembers initially resisting that idea because on page one of that story, a child is killed in a combine accident. He was concerned about that being the beginning of his book. "It was a very bold move, and it worried me at first," says Alan. But in the end, he realized it was a decision that helped shape not only the book's order, but also reader expectations. "It said to the reader, this is the world you are entering; if you make it through page one, then you're in."

That starting point also helped Alan crystallize his thinking for the whole arc of the book. He'd been cognizant of writing around themes of grief and injustice in general, but he hadn't thought about those themes across the entire collection. He certainly had to think about characters and plot points that were common to all the stories, but up to this point he hadn't considered how the stories interacted with each other on deeper levels. So in considering order, he found that the stories could speak to broader themes depending on where he placed them. If you make the tragic "Stained Freight" the first story, "you come to understand that these stories take people through grief and injustice into some kind of insight." That lens shaped the way he thought about the rest of the collection.

Our authors gave a lot of consideration to how thematic elements, whether tracked or found, drove their narratives. The critics might not care, but aspiring writers definitely should be thinking through their intentions.

Charting to Better Stories

Many of our authors mentioned outlining and storyboarding as part of their process. Some dove into outlining before they started, others after a first draft, still others in final revisions. Whatever the timing, they all used this method to test and refine key aspects of their manuscripts.

Storyboards are commonly used in film and picture books. A storyboard is a series of illustrations or sketches that help the creator visualize the structure of the story. Though some disagreement exists, the French filmmaker Georges Méliès is most often identified as the founder of storyboarding; the process helped him develop the famous 1902 film *A Trip to the Moon*.* In the 1930s Walt Disney Studios adopted the practice, which helped make it standard practice today in film and television development.

As this chapter shows, some authors have adapted the practice for their own story development. Writers such as Alan Heathcock and Courtney Maum draw rough sketches and summarize the basic action of their scenes on individual cards or sheets of paper. Sketches may be as simple as stick-figure drawings, but the drawing is an important part of the process. It allows the author to review plot points visually, spotting the gaps, so they can figure out what new directions might solve problems in the narrative.

Storyboarding is just one method of charting out your story. Our authors used outlines, charts, and storyboards to evaluate a number of different elements in their manuscripts. Here are some specific ways our authors used those charts to improve their stories.

Charting the Action

Every story can benefit from a look at each chapter from an action perspective. What's happening in a chapter or scene to change opinions, circumstances, desires, hopes, expectations, or outlooks? And if a given action doesn't accomplish any of those things, what is the purpose of the scene or chapter?

It's not that every chapter or scene needs to propel the story in a new direction, but asking if it does can be a good test. If it isn't propelling the story, what is it doing? Brian Benson's editor Denise Roy encouraged him to alternate between action and relationship chapters. The relationship chapters were important, but when they were stacked one upon another, the story stalled. So Brian needed

---

* Steven Price and Chris Pallant, *Storyboarding: A Critical History* (Houndmills, Basingstoke, UK: Palgrave Macmillan, 2015).

to plot out the flow and structure of his story and shake it up so the reader could experience the momentum that Brian intended.

Charting Complications

Whether nonfiction or fiction, story is compelling when the reader shares in the discovery and desires of the people on the page. If those elements don't change or complicate, the story stalls. Luckily, you can map out or storyboard your scenes and examine them with some simple conjunctions.

Write down a sentence to describe the action in each chapter or scene. If you can connect each with "and then," you've got a series of connected incidents. On the other hand, if you have no choice but to connect your scene or chapter sentences with "but then" or "and therefore," then you have a dynamic story complicated by the events and characters taking part in it. In case you're wondering, the latter is usually much better.

Charting Themes

Whether our authors set out to develop thematic elements or not, most ended up tracking and changing them in revision. Edan Lepucki didn't originally intend to make her story examine the role of secrets in a marriage. But in revision, after she'd noticed this theme come up several times, she looked through the rest of the manuscript for opportunities to play it up.

Some authors, like Edan, purposely wait until a book is complete before they outline, feeling that's the best time to enhance the themes. But whether it's at the beginning or at the end, tracking how thematic elements play out in a story can be a powerful exercise.

Charting Tension

Several of the authors spoke about tracking the tension of chapters or scenes throughout their books. They would come up with descriptive or even numbered scales to rate tension and try to ensure that the story has variety as it moves forward.

To a reader, it's just as boring if the story is nothing but high-intensity scenes as it is if they're all flat and tepid. The authors tried to break up the highest tension points of their books with moments of levity or other kinds of relief.

Charting Time

The final area where the authors used outlining or charting was in time and story threads. Several of the authors needed to tell stories with sequenced events, sometimes spanning long periods. In addition, some of the narratives braided between points in time as well as points of view.

In order to keep their story from falling off the rails, many re-ordered their narrative into a chronological outline. With that, they marked the actions that happened at various points and ensured they weren't crossing any wires as the story became more complex.

6. Reviewing Revision

"I believe more in the scissors than I do in the pencil," said Truman Capote.[1] Seek out guidance on revision, and this kind of wisdom tends to pop up. "My pencils outlast their erasers," said Vladimir Nabokov.[2] "Any story that's going to be any good is usually going to change," said Alice Munro.[3]

So revision is of primary importance, but other than the obvious point that a first draft needs a second look, what does that mean? How do writers go about revising their work most effectively?

More importantly, when does revision even begin? After all, it comes into the process at different stages and often involves other people such as critique partners, editors, or agents. Other times it is a deeply personal process involving painful decisions that others never know about. And while it almost inevitably means changes at the paragraph or sentence level, it can also involve restructuring the whole story, cutting or adding characters, and other major reconstructions.

No matter who or what it involves or when it takes place, revision always begins with some element of completed work—a chapter, a section, a manuscript—now ready for an opinion. That's why when it came to revision, there was one thing that all of our authors could agree on: get something down. Obviously if revision is the heart of the work, then you can't start it without something to react to. But most of the authors, in one way or another, argued that the most important stage in writing is getting to a point where you can consider revision.

That's a quiet victory. Once these writers reached the revision stage, they approached it in different ways. For some, certain core ideas or sections within the manuscript were untouchable. For others, anything was fair game in revision, and the process helped illuminate the aspects of the manuscript that were essential. Either way, there's a lot to learn from these authors about the revision process.

Finding the Core

Many of our authors learned revision the hard way—with little guidance, and through their own missteps. For many, it took stepping away from the manuscript—sometimes for days, sometimes for years—before they could return to it with ideas on how to solve the flaws. And sometimes it took outside feedback to help the author see their work in a new way.

Rebecca Makkai found a new direction to revise *The Borrower* after an inquiry from an agent whom Rebecca didn't ultimately work with. At the time Rebecca had left *The Borrower* behind, instead focusing on the manuscript which would ultimately become her second novel, *The Hundred-Year House*. She'd decided to move forward, resigned to the possibility that *The Borrower* might be the first-novel-in-a-drawer that so many authors talk about. So when she reached the stage of querying agents, she did so for *The Hundred-Year House* manuscript.

She received a positive response from an early query, but the agent told Rebecca that while she loved her writing and loved her short stories, she didn't love *The Hundred-Year House*. The agent then asked if Rebecca had anything else to share. Though her draft of *The Borrower* was mostly done, Rebecca knew it wasn't ready to share with the outside world. "So I went on this mad revision quest, and as

I returned to it and started revising, I realized that it really was the book that I wanted to work on. It was in such better shape than my second book."

Because of that one outside push, Rebecca's whole outlook shifted. She started to see the strengths in *The Borrower* and became excited about the possibilities in revision. The manuscript still had major flaws, so Rebecca turned her attention to addressing them. "It was this long chain of being in love with this novel, breaking up with this novel, looking back at it realizing that there was really something there, returning to it, getting frustrated, abandoning it again, in many different stages, but finally finding that spark again and committing myself to finishing it."

The conversation with that agent reignited her commitment, but she needed a writing breakthrough before being ready to move forward. It happened in reviewing her prologue. In the published prologue, which hasn't changed much from the original version, the main character Lucy Hull begins by positioning herself between "Huck and Humbert." That's Huckleberry Finn and Humbert Humbert from *Lolita*.

Rebecca knew all along that her book held echoes of canonical works in which children embark on questionable journeys with adults. But in the original manuscript, the point of departure stymied the momentum of her narrative. So after reading that line in the prologue, Rebecca went back and reviewed *The Adventures of Huckleberry Finn* and *Lolita*.

She realized in reading them that there was one major difference between their narrative structures, and that difference lit her way forward. "In *Huck Finn*, you have Huck and Jim going down the river on this raft, and as flawless as it is, the one criticism that people have is that they get onto the river and it is too episodic. In *Lolita*, likewise, some of the tension goes out of the book when Humbert and Lolita take off together. And I realized that what Nabokov does is introduce a third party, this character named Quilty, who follows them around."

At the same time, Rebecca was attempting to write a synopsis for her book. In retrospect, she says she recommends that all writers, especially those working on their first novel, write a synopsis before they try to finish it. "Suddenly when you're looking at the plot over one page instead of three hundred pages, the gaps in it become utterly clear. The synopsis basically said, 'And then they get on the road and go a bunch of places.' So I found myself typing into the synopsis, 'They found themselves being followed,' which was not something I had written into the actual book at all."

Rebecca had a lot of work to do to introduce this change into her manuscript, but that was the moment when it clicked for her. She knew how to finish her story and she set out to do it. She didn't end up working with the agent who reached out to her, but she credits that moment for helping her find the core of her story. "I've now realized that it is very hard to write a two-character novel. Even harder when those two characters are largely aligned in their intentions. So triangulating, introducing a third point, something for [Lucy] to worry about and draw her away from Ian—that really helped get the story done."

External pushes like the one that helped Rebecca finish *The Borrower* are powerful, and they're why aspiring authors should try to find "pushers." Another external push helped one of our authors wipe off ten years of dust and dig in. Pause for a second and think about that. Ten years prior, Courtney Maum had literally put the *I Am Having So Much Fun Here without You* manuscript in a box. She was abandoning it, certain she'd never return.

But Courtney had started working with the literary agent Rebecca Gradinger on another manuscript. As they worked together, it became clear that that book might need to wait. Rebecca didn't think they could sell the manuscript—not as a debut novel—but she hadn't signed Courtney based solely on that project. In a shift from some of our other authors' experiences (which will be recounted in a later chapter), when that project stalled, Rebecca didn't drop Courtney; she asked her what was next. She told Courtney that she wanted to work with her across her career, not just on one project. "I was just so impressed with Courtney's voice, and her talent, and I knew from reading everything she had shared with me that I wanted to work with her," recalls Rebecca.

Rebecca admits this is somewhat unusual. If an agent and author start off working on a book that eventually withers, that often means their relationship is over. Rebecca knew she wanted to work with Courtney long term, but she also felt they needed to find the right project for Courtney's debut novel.

Courtney had already made peace with the idea that *I Am Having So Much Fun Here without You*, then titled *The Blue Bear*, would never see the light of day. In her mind, it didn't really register as a possibility. It was a first, failed novel attempt that she had mourned and moved on from. So when Rebecca asked her for any other work, it took her awhile to even admit she had this decade-old manuscript sitting in a box.

Courtney says that some small part of her still believed in the story, but she mostly considered the old manuscript "naive and contrived." She felt so certain that Rebecca would read it and reject it that she just sent it as it was, without even rereading it. But Rebecca read it in a slightly different way than she would read most other manuscripts. "I knew where she was as a writer ten years later. So I gave it a wide berth. I understood and was excited to see what she could bring to it."

So the old draft needed lots of work and had plenty of flaws, but Rebecca knew Courtney had the experience and skills to address them. Rebecca looked past the flaws in a way she normally wouldn't with standard queries that come across her desk. "Sometimes I'll read something and I'll admire it a lot, but I won't have that sort of visceral connection where I feel like I need to pick up a pen and start editing it. Much of my job at the beginning with any client is helping them get that manuscript into a shape where you can take it out and show it to editors. There was something in Courtney's story that sparked that connection for me."

Rebecca thinks Courtney was too hard on herself when she said that ten-year-old manuscript was naive and contrived. "There were certainly parts that needed work, but it was a first draft, and many writers of incredible talent start with a very flawed manuscript," says Rebecca. "They say that writing is revision, and it's really true."

Courtney didn't expect Rebecca to like the draft, so when Rebecca reached out to say "This is it, this is your debut novel," she wasn't immediately on board. "I had to convince her," says Rebecca. "She put me through the paces, asking, 'Well, why? What do you see in this?'"

Over several conversations, Courtney's resistance began to fade, especially as she went back to the manuscript and read it through in the light of Rebecca's enthusiasm. She remembers slowly rediscovering aspects of the manuscript that she had always loved. As Courtney came around to the idea, she still understood that the work wasn't ready. So she and Rebecca discussed the aspects of the novel that needed to change, and she dove in.

Rebecca says one of the things that makes Courtney different from some writers is that she listens more than most when it comes to revision. Courtney doesn't just make the suggested change; she wants to understand the reason behind it, so she can consider other ways to approach it. "Courtney is able to go away, think about what I've said, and then revise and deliver something that's wholly new, and even better than I imagined," says Rebecca.

Courtney took Rebecca's suggestions and notes and went back to the manuscript. But she knew that just tinkering with a decade-old manuscript wasn't the path forward. So she took the structure and ideas from the first manuscript and built an outline from it. Then she put that old draft back in the box where it came from and began rewriting the entire story from scratch. After her first time through that old draft, she never returned to it during the entire process of writing the new manuscript. "I didn't even want it in the same room with me," she says. "I knew it well enough, those people were in my head, and I knew what I was trying to accomplish. But it just hurt too much to look at hundreds of thousands of words and think, 'Oh, that was for nothing.' If I can't see the draft—if I'm just working out a mood I want—then I can rewrite it without feeling resentment."

The time between the first manuscript and the second one gave Courtney new perspective. The core of her story didn't change between the drafts, but her understanding of human relationships had deepened. She says for a story that revolved around a marriage, the first draft was too one-dimensional. "In comparison to the original draft, the portrait of their marriage became more loving and realistic. I'd written the first draft with him treating his wife like this ball on the end of a chain that he couldn't wait to get rid of. When I wrote it, I wasn't married myself, and I just thought, 'Well, of course, after seven years with the same person you're going to want to cheat, and you'd feel like you had permission to.'"

Courtney is careful to point out that a writer doesn't need to live every experience they try to write about, but it's important to have enough experience that it becomes translatable. "It took being married myself to understand how close resentment and love can be to each other," she says.

The marriage in her story needed to be more complicated, and it needed to demonstrate more empathy and purpose and will and responsibility for everyone involved. "When a relationship falls apart, even if someone is more a victim, it still happens between two people, and I worked really hard to show that for this particular couple. Especially with a child involved, I just needed to be more compassionate to everyone in the story."

In her rereading of the original manuscript, one of the things that most surprised Courtney was how poorly the wife character, Anne, came across. She wasn't the point-of-view character, but Courtney had always assumed she'd be a sympathetic character. After all, she's the scorned wife with the cheating husband. But Courtney had portrayed her as overly angry and one-dimensional. As she reread, Courtney thought, "'Why the hell *wouldn't* he cheat on this killjoy?' So I had to work hard to make her a more complicated character too. One you weren't necessarily rooting for either, but that you felt compassion toward, and also maybe didn't quite trust 100 percent. Maybe she is seeing someone on the side too. I had to make her as complicated as she deserved to be, and not just be this one-dimensional slighted woman, which didn't interest me at all."

Rebecca Gradinger was really impressed with the revised manuscript after Courtney submitted it. More, she admired Courtney's work ethic when it came to revision. Rebecca thinks it's something other writers could learn from and emulate. Courtney doesn't tinker or fume; she tries to understand the feedback, what it is that isn't working, and then to address the underlying issue in order to make her manuscript as strong as possible. "She'll tell you she hates revision, but she does it," says Rebecca. "Much more than many people. She'll send me something and be happy about it for two days, and then you call her on that third day, and she's knee deep in it, making it better again."

Rebecca Makkai and Courtney Maum needed an external push in order to find the core of their work. But they also needed time away from it. And while Edan Lepucki and Monona Wali didn't get the same push, they too needed significant time away before being able to revise their manuscripts.

Monona finished the draft of her story quickly, in about six months. But it took her many attempts—including major revisions and many breaks from the manuscript—before she was ready to publish it. "The arc of the story was there from the beginning," she says. "But I hadn't fully developed it, so it really was a two-part process."

Monona's strategy was to write what she could, get the story down without a lot of plotting, then address holes in plot and story. She took breaks from the work over substantial stretches of time, then returned to it and identified the areas that needed the most attention. She says that this method has always been part of her process. If she doesn't have distance from her manuscript, she has trouble identifying the gaps and problems.

Edan Lepucki had a similar approach. As you'll recall from the origins chapter, Edan attended the UCross Fellowship having just learned that her agent was dropping her and her still unpublished book. So she turned to writing *California* at the fellowship. Edan finished a full draft several months later, but many more months passed before she showed it to anyone.

She says she's learned since her experience with *California* that it takes her about two years of tinkering on a draft before she feels ready for others to weigh in and help her shape it further. And even then, she says, the draft is still a mess. "It usually has large structural issues but really pretty sentences. I really like sentences. I like to say it's sort of like a Barbie—it looks really good, but it can't stand up."

As you may recall, Edan is more of an organic writer than an outliner, and this means the issue she most needs to address in revision is structure. Her sentences and even chapters may work well as individual units, but the framework needs work in order for it to all come together in harmony.

Having worked with many writing students, she knows revision is a very personal process. But one strategy that continues to work well for her, and one she recommends to her students, is to take time away before jumping into the revision process. The distance consistently helps you see the strengths and flaws with fresh eyes. "You can read it like a reader again, not the person writing it," says Edan.

Addressing Feedback

Pushed or not, time away or not, deciding to share your work is a big moment for any writer. Whether you're sharing with an editor, agent, mentor, teacher, friend, spouse, or parent, it's tough to do. It doesn't mean an author wipes their hands and says, "All done," but it does signify a perceived readiness. When and how to approach this is an intensely personal decision for each writer, and while there isn't necessarily one right way to seek feedback, we can learn significant lessons from how our authors handled it with their debut books.

Cynthia Bond was not surprised by the feedback she received, but that didn't mean it didn't sting a little. She'd already heard from a few people that her manuscript was pretty long, maybe too long, but then her agent Nicole Aragi got back to her. She'd read through the entire nine-hundred-page manuscript. Nicole had a number of suggestions in her notes to Cynthia, but her most significant note said, "This is more than one book."

Cynthia remembers that her first reaction was complete resistance, a reaction she now advises against. "Prepare yourself before you get feedback," she says. "Otherwise you go into auto-resistance."

But she'd put a lot of work into creating this massive manuscript — all those clotheslines of notes strung between her work-desk pillars. And that one little sentence from her agent meant she'd have to string them back up and reshuffle the whole manuscript. Splitting it up didn't just mean ending it a third of the way through and calling the first book done; it meant reworking the entire manuscript into three coherent and self-sustaining stories.

Her resistance stayed intact for about a night, but then it faded as she considered it more. "Sometimes you hear things and they resonate in your body, like down to your bones, and even as I resisted, I knew she was right," says Cynthia. "A very important thing for new writers to hear is that you've got to be malleable. If you feel like something really can't change, that someone wants to change the soul of your book, then you have to stand up for that. But you've also got to be open to criticism."

Even though it took her a day or two to remember those lessons, Cynthia says she had learned about flexibility through years of teaching, theater, and academic pursuits. Ultimately she found a way to accept the feedback and get to work on reinventing her story as a trilogy.

Brian Benson was newer to writing and critique, so he had quite a bit to learn in terms of dealing with feedback. His first and maybe most important lesson was that even though his story was about him, the Brian on the page was still a character in a story to his readers. And after hearing feedback he realized his first draft wasn't portraying that character in the best light.

"I have this tendency to be overly self-deprecating to the point of sarcasm," explains Brian. "And that's still very much part of the book, because I believe in being critical of myself, I think it's something we don't always do enough. But it needs the right balance. I also needed to address the ways in which I respect myself and the positive ways in which people see me."

Brian's first reader was his friend Galen, who is also a key figure in the book. Galen sat down with Brian to talk through the section he'd read. He started with the good, telling Brian it was funny and engaging, and he wanted to read more. But then he delivered the tough news. "He said, 'If you keep writing it this way, everyone is going to hate you,'" says Brian.

When Brian joined the Attic's Atheneum program and worked with Cheryl Strayed and Karen Karbo, this lesson was reinforced. Like any great character in fiction, the character of the memoirist needs to be flawed and vulnerable but also robust and empathetic. He'd done the flawed and vulnerable work, but the Brian on the page came off flat and even a little pathetic. Brian had a lot of work to do. Not only did he need to change the way he was writing, but he had to figure out the positive parts of the story he had left out. He could keep the moments of doubt and self-deprecating humor, but he also needed to show moments of growth, determination, and grit as he continued on the cross-country bike journey.

The other key thing Brian learned from early feedback was that he had a tendency to be overly internal. "You know, all my thoughts and feelings," explains Brian. "But that's not what I or anyone likes to read. I like to read a story where I can feel it and see it." When he worked on one of his chapters with Karen Karbo, she challenged him to use all five senses in every paragraph of the whole chapter. "Practically speaking, you can't do that, but having that thought in my mind was tremendously helpful as I worked on revising the book and making it more external," says Brian.

The last major problem Brian recalls working on in revision is one that can hamstring many writers. In his first draft, he tended to broadcast what was coming without letting the story unfold organically for the reader. "I had forecast everything that was wrong with Rachel's and my relationship right at the beginning of the book, before even any mention of us getting out on the road. So I had some early readers say, 'This is a little heavy for page 14—you might want to hold some of these details back.'"

So Brian had to think more about how the story would progress. Instead of catching readers up to his state of mind in the present, he needed to tell them about his state of mind when he began the journey. That backstory, that changing state of mind and relationship, would more naturally slip in and out as the journey on the page progressed. As he addressed these aspects, his story continued to evolve and change. "The outline I ended with is kind of like the bike trip itself. I had a destination in mind, but I kept getting detoured over and over again as I went."

The feedback Brian heard helped him develop the tone and scope of his narrative and helped him more deeply understand the nature of memoir in general. Our other memoirist, Clara Bensen, came to some of the same lessons a little further into her process. Her viral article and quick book deal meant that not only was she not used to grappling with feedback but she wasn't even sure where to find it. It's why she ultimately decided to work with a freelance editor, Abe Louise Young, a decision discussed in the support chapter. Clara was initially fairly resistant to showing her work to anyone, even her agent or editor.

But she soon came to value that external perspective. "I tend to be very intense and neurotic," says Clara. "So my head is often in outer space. I need to be brought back down to earth so that I'm communicating what I want. The feedback helped me make my writing more potent."

One of the chief things that came up during revisions with Abe Louise Young was that the character of Jeff needed work. Jeff has a daughter and is a well-known figure in the Austin, Texas, community where both he and Clara still live. So Clara felt very protective of him as she started writing. She also didn't want the book to harm their still-undefined relationship. "So his character in the early drafts came off as an angelic caricature, and I had to go back through and make him more human—to show his weaknesses and faults."

In all of the cases so far, the authors found helpful feedback and incorporated it. But another lesson became clear in talking to our authors: sometimes when it comes to feedback, you need to develop the skill to sort the wheat from the chaff.

Eric Smith, author of *Inked*, learned early on in his publishing career that sometimes advice or feedback is just a matter of taste. He urges fellow writers to trust their instincts and make the edits that make sense to their own vision for the work. Eric says that if you start to see a trend in the feedback, then you need to rethink. "Just because one person dislikes something doesn't mean an entire audience of readers will. But if you start hearing the same thing from a lot of readers, then you need to revisit it. There's a big difference between sticking to your guns and just being stubborn."

Monona Wali had to learn the hard way to trust her instincts. I'll explore that in depth in the next section, but for her the lesson was invaluable. "When you're starting out, you don't necessarily have that confidence," she says. "But you need to find it, or you can get led astray."

Zetta Elliott had found that confidence and, as a young writer, stood up for the vision behind her work. "I would say my general feeling about my books is that I'm not interested in doing a rewrite. I will revise, of course, but I don't write for hire. I think it's one of the biggest frustrations in working with publishers. A lot of times an editor sees a kernel in a story and thinks that they can shape it into something else entirely."

Early on, Zetta worked with an editor who sent her an editorial letter that asked her to change her story to target an older age group because *Bird* was too much about drugs and death. "But it's *not* a book about drugs and death, and I knew that," says Zetta. "It's a book about how a child uses art to memorialize a lost loved one and to transcend grief."

Zetta had written in the picture-book format precisely because she wanted to reach younger kids. The requested change might have worked for an entirely different manuscript, but it violated Zetta's core purpose in writing this story.

For her, writing *Bird* was an avenue to help kids have productive conversations about tough issues such as addiction and loss. The publisher who wrote her that letter was a white woman who didn't share the same life experiences as Zetta, and Zetta felt the request was an example of a privileged and often culturally insensitive publishing industry. She knows from her own family and work experiences that "many kids know prematurely about addiction." And no one was really talking to them about it, especially not in picture books.

She saw the request to "age up" her story as coming from someone who'd had the privilege of never seeing or experiencing those situations as a child. The request created a dilemma for Zetta. "I definitely talked to some of my writer friends, and they asked me to think about the ask and how important it was to me. At the time I'd worked with urban kids for years, and many of them know far too prematurely the effects of addiction. I just wasn't going to age it up for no reason."

So although she likely could have found a publisher for a chapter-book version of *Bird*, she decided she'd rather leave it unpublished than change the core of it. Fortunately, that's not what happened.

She worked on some of the other requested revisions but maintained the picture-book length and format. That ultimately meant closing the door on working with that editor, and that might have been it for the book, but as we'll see in the next chapter, a set of illustrations helped convince another editor that this book could be powerful for the intended age group as it was written.

But when Zetta made the decision, she wasn't sure if *Bird* would ever see the light of day. It was a big decision, to possibly sink her book rather than change it, and the experience has stuck with her. Since *Bird* came out, Zetta has self-published the great majority of her work.

Working with the Pros

Working through revision with a trusted reader, a spouse, friend, parent, or writing group is great and serves writers well. But eventually most pieces of writing have to be seen by someone who works on manuscripts for a living, usually an agent, an editor, or both. (The next chapter addresses how such people come into the picture.)

Sometimes the feedback from professionals is difficult to hear and challenging to carry out. But finding the best ways to work with such feedback was important for our authors. The early versions of Eric Smith's *Inked* began with a prologue. It served as a note to the reader from Caenum, the main character and point-of-view voice, and started with the line "Ink, like the Fate it inevitably determines, is a funny thing." That line survived version after version—writing group, agent, and critique partner—but in the final edit with Bloomsbury Spark editor Meredith Rich, the line got cut along with the entire prologue.

The line survived so long because it works on many levels. It prepares the reader for the book's premise while opening up a number of necessary questions. Plus there's something subversive in the subtext. When a broad or personal concept like luck or love or fate is described as funny, we often mean it's unpredictable or maybe a little unfair. But with that one short sentence, Eric had revealed that in the world of this book, even fated ends can't be predicted.

As a solo line, a reader might argue for Eric's original in favor of the book's new first line, "Three days." So why cut a powerful first line in favor of one that's more ordinary? Don't writers want to knock readers on their ass with their first line and never let them back up? Well, edits at this stage need to consider every aspect of the manuscript, not just the sentence level or first impression. After reading multiple versions of his beginning chapter, Eric could see that the final edited version is the strongest.

Any writing choice, and the why behind it, is important. But when the why question is asked in isolation, it leads to a simplistic answer. No writing choice is made in a vacuum, and one of the best lessons a young writer can learn is the importance of context.

The oft-repeated advice in writing workshops to "kill your darlings" is usually attributed to William Faulkner. In fact, Faulkner popularized the idea, but he didn't come up with it. Sir Arthur Quiller-Couch gave a series of lectures on writing at Cambridge in 1914. In his lecture on style, Quiller-Couch said, "Whenever you feel an impulse to perpetrate a piece of exceptionally fine writing, obey it—whole-heartedly—and delete it before sending your manuscript to press. Murder your darlings."[4]

Of course this isn't meant as blanket advice. It doesn't mean delete all your best work; it means cut the things that you love if they aren't improving or helping your story. So back to Eric Smith's original first line and prologue: it may have done some work in shaping the story for the reader, and it was a strong line on its own, but in the end it wasn't serving the novel as a whole.

In the initial version of *Inked*, the main character, Caenum, is consumed with the coming of the Chill, a deep freeze across the land. He's overwhelmed with how it will impact his father and his town. The final edited version of the book doesn't omit the Chill, but it comes into play much later. The story's original beginning focused too much on the external and not enough on Caenum.

Eric explains, "While I really like selfless characters that focus on bigger pictures, in the end we aren't perfect. That's what makes a good YA story: flawed characters that grow. So narrowing his perspective a little was important." The broad scope of that initial line no longer served the story, and as strong as it was, as hard as it was, Eric needed to cut it.

Instead of the Chill, Eric focused on the three days Caenum had left before his Inking. In the world of *Inked* every person must get a tattoo at eighteen, called the Inking, which determines their role for the rest of their life. Unlike in our world, where tattoos can be seen as rebellious, in this world tattoos are order and tradition. Caenum's growing dread of the Inking is much more pronounced in the edited version of the book. Eric says, "Focusing on what was happening to him and the whole Inking ordeal was important, because it makes for a bigger story when he realizes how it affects other people much later."

No facts or events really changed between the various versions, but the focus shifted from Caenum's external world to his inner one, and that shift allows the reader to connect with Caenum more closely from the get-go. The two versions now read like different translations of the same work—in fact, Eric says that the trick between author, editor, and agent is to find the best possible "translation" for the book.

And what about that beautiful prologue? "It was one of those ideas I really liked and thought was fun, but it had to go to serve the story. Which is fine. Maybe it'll end up in an e-book prequel or something. A boy can dream, right?"

Serving the story instead of ego was a common theme among the lessons these authors said they took away from their editorial process. Graduating from the most prestigious MFA program in the country, Edan Lepucki was used to responding to rigorous feedback, but even she struggled with the editorial letter she received about *California* from her editor, Allie Sommer, at Little, Brown. "It was so long and so intense, I actually burst out crying. And it wasn't because I didn't think she understood me; it was that I knew she was right about everything."

Edan says that letter also helped her in her work as a writing teacher. She'd been leading workshops for years by the time she received it, but she'd become somewhat inured to criticism and feedback. So it was a good reminder about how to give and receive feedback at certain points in a project. "It had been a long time since I had felt that much in the hot seat, and it reminded me how intense that can be. Even with feedback that you respect and are so grateful for, it is really intense."

But with her initial reaction behind her, Edan realized she had no choice but to get to work. There were several minor suggestions, but the two main issues she needed to figure out were cutting some initial flashbacks and more fully considering the world these characters inhabited. Her first draft had far too many flashbacks at the beginning, which slowed down the narrative. But those flashbacks needed to be present somewhere, because they were crucial to how the story developed. Edan had to reconstruct almost every section of the manuscript so that they could come in later.

For her world building, Edan's editor encouraged her to see through the characters' eyes. "I would have random things about

China or some other part of the international stage, and my editor pointed out that 'either you have to really go in and explain this, or we need to cut it.' She rightly said that we needed to strike a balance between what the characters would realistically know about the world and the reader's desire to know what was going on."

Alan Heathcock was relieved and thrilled to sell *Volt* to Graywolf. "Everything you do as a writer is kind of on faith because you don't get paid until it's done, and I don't think there are many other things that work that way. It's an insanity. So when I sold it, it was a tremendous relief based on all the sacrifices my family had made."

But the next day Alan came to a rather stark realization. This wasn't the end point—it was the beginning of his revision work. "I knew I then had to get these stories ready for the world. And they had to be impeccable and precise. I didn't want to have the slightest regret of having this go out into the world and feel like I did not do something to get it absolutely ready."

So what did that mean for Alan? He needed to write a story or two to complete the collection, but more than anything, he needed to go through the stories that had already been published in a number of prestigious journals and make sure that as a whole they would come together well for the reader. "I had to understand each story as a unit of communication," Alan says. Even if a story stood just fine on its own, it might not stand in relation to the other stories, so Alan had to do a lot of work to line them up.

During this process he received revision notes from his editor, Fiona McCrae, at Graywolf. She challenged some of his thinking about manuscript cohesion, in particular his ideas for the manuscript order.

Alan says hearing that feedback was hard. Part of him wanted to resist every suggestion that didn't line up with his own ideas, and part of him wanted to just do whatever Graywolf had said, but he came to a middle ground as he worked on it. "I wanted the reading experience to be potent, and this intense process made me a much better writer. I took each story and first asked myself what I wanted to accomplish. Then I considered my own notes and the notes from my editor, and asked myself, 'Do the suggestions here enhance the goal of each story?'"

Alan came to two realizations as he worked through this process. Number one, identifying the communication goal of each story helped him see them much more clearly. And second, he let go of any aspect of ego associated with each story. He wrote and revised to try to reach those goals, and he didn't care where the suggestion came from that helped him get there.

Brian Benson also found that letting go of ego was helpful in working with his editor, Denise Roy at Plume. In their initial work together, they shared one specific goal: cutting. The manuscript that Brian sold was about 122,000 words, but the contract that he'd signed called for it to be 85,000 words, so he and Denise sat down and talked about areas that could be trimmed. He says Denise was particularly good at identifying patterns in the book where certain things were repeatedly rehashed.

But once the manuscript was shortened, there was still work to do, and this part was more challenging. Denise pushed Brian to think about the overarching flow of the story and how the chapters played off each other. "She'd say something like 'Here we've had three relationship chapters in a row, so right now we need an action chapter.' My initial impulse was 'Well, but that's not how it played out in real life.'"

Brian's instincts were toward telling the story in the order he remembered it, but he now understands that Denise was pushing him away from his chronological memory and toward telling the story as well as possible. It was a shift for Brian to think about the story with a focus on the reader instead of simply "how it happened."

Changing a chapter's focus from relationship introspection to exterior action didn't actually change the accuracy of his story. It just changed the order in which those events were revealed to the reader and helped propel the narrative so the reader didn't start to feel stuck. "What I really learned the most from Denise is the flow and pacing a book needs to have. You need to modulate to keep a reader's interest. Just because you had a strong feeling in a given moment doesn't mean that's how the light needs to shine on the page. So a lot of my revision involved getting out of my internal head space and into others' experiences. I had to meld the external world with my own experience."

Brian also learned some lessons about structure and revision from his agent. As he revised in preparation for finding a publisher, he had operated under the assumption that he could always go back and change what he was writing. It helped him move forward with his work and not get too stuck in the decision-making process. But it also had implications he hadn't fully considered.

After he'd started working with his agent, David Forrer, they wrote a proposal for *Going Somewhere* and started shopping it around. The early chapters that Brian had written, combined with the planned structure in the book proposal, started to lock him into a specific direction for his book. Once the book drew interest and sold based on some of the premises in that proposal, he realized it was likely too late to go back and change any of those major premises.

The book proposal was primarily for a story about the bike trip, so any other topics Brian thought about including needed to go. And while that *was* the book he had intended to write, realizing he was completely locked into that focus threw him off. He feared it would limit the ways he could tell his story. But as he worked on it, he came to realize that this is the nature of every book-publishing experience. "At a certain point you just have to make peace with the fact that you've chosen to write the book this way. Every kind of structure opens up some doors and closes others. So accepting that and moving forward was a big part of my process in revision."

So some authors found professional help with editors after their books sold, but what about the writers who sought this kind of help before they sold their work? Monona Wali decided to hire some help for *My Blue Skin Lover*. She found a renowned editor and got back a number of good edits, but in the end, this input didn't work for her and it set her project back.

The editor Monona hired had a great reputation, so Monona hired him without really thinking about whether their styles were a good fit. At the time she was receiving rejections from a number of agents. So she listened to the advice of her hired editor and changed the story to a kind of book he said would sell better. She expanded her 150-page manuscript to more than 300 pages. "In the end, though, I think my instincts for this book were right from the get-go. The manuscript had a very poetic, lyrical feel, and it needed to be the length that it is. It didn't need to be this big fat novel."

Monona doesn't blame the editor; he just wasn't a good fit. She still believes that hiring an editor can be helpful, but only if you do your homework. You need to do more than just look at reputations, she says—you need to look for a good fit for your project, and ask the editor tough questions. If you don't, you may spend unnecessary money and waste a lot of time moving your book in a direction you don't believe in.

That experience sidetracked Monona's manuscript for about two years. When she got it back to a form she was comfortable with, her next major revision was to develop the secondary characters, which was a big help to the book. This strategy had emerged during her work with the hired editor, so while parts of the process set her back, it did help her improve the manuscript.

We've explored some of Monona's secondary character additions already, but another key addition was the character called Jangles. The story needed a more grounded beginning and an event that would propel the narrative. So Monona invented the character of Jangles, whose heart attack in the street kicks off the central chain of events in the novel. That event also allowed Monona to bring the character of Shiva into the narrative much earlier. It was a big addition that required a lot of revision, but it ultimately strengthened her entire story.

Delilah Dawson worked rather extensively with her agent, Kate McKean, before submitting her manuscript to publishers. Kate sent Delilah multiple letters with feedback. One such letter, fourteen pages long, actually led Delilah to a moment of tears. It was a lot to take in, an issue that will be taken up in the setbacks chapter. But after taking a day or two to recover, Delilah pushed herself forward and worked on revising the whole first half of her manuscript.

Kate knows that moment was hard for Delilah, particularly because the letter asked her to make significant changes to her main character. But despite the difficulty and perhaps a few gnashed teeth, Kate could see the difference as Delilah revised. "Delilah has always been a fast learner," says Kate. "The next draft was better, and then the next and the next. As I read more of her work, I saw her incorporating what we'd talked about, and it was immensely gratifying—not only because her subsequent first drafts were better and didn't require several rounds of editing for both of us, but because she was learning and I could see it."

Delilah echoes Kate's thoughts about her work. She says that letter was hard, but Kate has made all the difference in helping her advance as a writer. Delilah says that no matter how hard it may be, if you don't try to learn from your drafts and apply that knowledge down the road, you're just spinning your wheels as a writer.

Revision Is Hard

No matter what was asked of them, all of our authors said revision is one of the hardest parts of writing. Some used more colorful words than that to describe the immense challenge. It's why many of them recommend writing a first draft as quickly as possible and then starting revisions. A first draft gives you something to react to, and as many of the authors pointed out, the sooner you can get to the revision stage, the sooner you'll get to the heart of writing your book.

But the bottom line is, revision can be gut-wrenching. It takes an open mind and the ability to see your work with new eyes. It's helpful to learn some of the strategies these authors did: finding the core of the work, when to step away from the work, when to seek feedback and how to deal with it, and how to find fresh perspective. As useful as those lessons are, the authors emphasized that revision is hard and personal no matter how refined your tactics are. Many of the authors also said that despite their hopes to the contrary, revision doesn't get easier after the first book is published.

Courtney Maum said it the most plainly. "Revision is a nightmare. Once your book comes out, people interview you as if you were a novelist, as if you've got everything down. And it's nice to be interviewed, so you speak like you know what you're talking about. But now I'm working on my second book, and once I started revising it, I said to myself, 'Oh, wait, I actually don't know anything about my writing process at all.' I'm still figuring it out, and quite a bit of it is a mess."

Revision Tactics

Here are several ideas, tactics, and resources for revision that came up during my interviews with our authors. You can experiment with these as you develop your own revision approach.

Let It Breathe

Many of our authors spoke of the book *The Artful Edit* by Susan Bell with fondness.[*] It brings together tips, exercises, and interviews to explore best approaches in revising and editing creative work. Among other ideas, it urges letting the draft sit, unattended for a while, before you return to it for revision.

Introduce All the Senses

In revising, sometimes the goal is to bring the reader closer in and make the writing less dry. Brian Benson used the advice in Steve Almond's book *This Won't Just Take But a Minute, Honey* to try to bring all five senses into every paragraph.[†] You can't reasonably do that, he says, but just having that as a goal helped him tremendously as he revised his book.

---

[*] Susan Bell, *The Artful Edit: On the Practice of Editing Yourself* (repr., New York: W. W. Norton, 2008).
[†] Steve Almond, *This Won't Take But a Minute, Honey* (Cambridge, MA: Author, n.d.).

Be Open

Revision is hard, and sometimes criticism is even harder. But your work can't get better if you shut it out or down. Many of our authors said they needed to learn how and when to take advice and criticism and how to work it into their books. As Cynthia Bond recommended, "Tuck your ego away or tell it to sit far away in a chair somewhere."

Start Big

It's the whole forest-and-trees idea. Revision isn't just copyediting and hunting for grammar mistakes. It's about evaluating the whole picture. Many of our authors needed to make big changes to their work. They said writers have to be careful not to waste time tinkering with sentences in a chapter or section that may be cut later. It could be a complete waste of time.

But Don't Forget the Details

Grammar, spelling, punctuation, diction, rhythm, clarity, and concision: don't forget to focus on these toward the end. Strunk and White's *Elements of Style* and William Zinsser's *On Writing Well* are classics for a reason, and many of the writers mentioned rereading these books from time to time.

7. Publishing Paths

There's a moment in every project—sometimes entirely premature, sometimes long overdue—when a writer sets aside the many shades of doubt and tries to find the book a home. As we'll see, the footing here can be rocky or steady, but the fog of ever-shifting publishing possibilities can obscure even the most certain path.

For our authors, whether they sought representation and traditional publication or took the self-publishing route, it helped to start with an ultimate vision for their work. Rejection is commonplace for writers, and with the growing number of viable publishing options, it can be easy to grasp at the first positive signal. Writers with a strong and cohesive vision for their work were better able to evaluate the options that arose and make tough decisions.

Based on their experiences, several of the writers profiled here cautioned against leaping at the first offer. Because they didn't yet have a clear vision for their book, they hadn't considered the element of fit, and their eagerness turned into regret down the line. When everything worked well, either by luck or by research, it worked because the authors found themselves paired with publishing partners that fit their work.

Deciding to seek an agent and choosing a publishing path came down to a few key considerations for these authors: audience, publishing freedom, and interest or willingness to take care of the business side of things. While there isn't one obvious path that makes sense for everyone, the stories from our authors highlight potential strategies and pitfalls among the options available to modern authors.

Our authors pursued a variety of publishing paths. But whether they self-published from the beginning, somewhere down the line, or not at all, most of the authors profiled for this book sought representation from a literary agent for their debut work. They shared a belief that it was the best possible route to get their work into the most hands. Still, as we'll see, for those who did find agents, that moment didn't result in easy success.

When Lightning Strikes

It's a big deal when a respected agent reaches out and says they believe enough in your writing to represent you. It means validation, new challenges, and the possibility of selling your book to a publisher (a process that will be covered in chapter 10).

Most of the agented authors had to first decide they were ready to start working with an agent. Clara Bensen is a different story, one that might incite some envy. That's because Clara had agents reaching out to her before she ever intended to write a book.

But that doesn't mean everything was easy for her. After her *Salon* article went viral, the calls began. "I totally walked into this thing without any clue what was about to happen," says Clara. "I never intended to write a book; it hadn't even passed through my mind, even after it all started going nuts. So when agents started emailing me to ask if I thought there was a bigger story here and whether I could write a whole book, I felt like I'd misread it, and then almost immediately afterward said, 'Ummm, yeah, of course I can write a book.'"

Clara began weighing her options regarding agents. Though she hadn't written a word of the book, Clara had a clear vision for the project. Some of the agents who contacted her saw it as a romantic beach read; they asked her to consider writing a longer version of her article. But Clara had other ideas. She knew there were elements in her story that fit that vision, but she felt playing them up would betray the big picture. A purely whimsical, easy-read memoir wouldn't reflect the mental health struggles that, as previously noted, were a large part of her untold story.

Clara started sorting through the inquiries, and she began to tell the agents her ideas for the book. She was confident enough to weed out the ones who weren't open to her vision. Eventually it came down to three agents, all of whom she liked very much. She decided to work with Stacy Testa at Writers House for three reasons. First, she felt that she and Stacy connected around the project. Second, Clara asked other writers she knew, and they all spoke highly of Stacy's literary agency. And finally, she and Stacy were about the same age, which was a big factor for Clara. "She's young in her career too, so I knew she'd be driven and have time and energy that someone with a bunch more authors might not. I wanted to try this with someone who was trying to launch their career as well."

Stacy Testa says that she reached out to Clara because she felt a connection with her initial story. When Clara told her about her broader ideas for it, she was excited about the possibilities. She also says she was undaunted by Clara's inexperience as a writer. "I'm a young agent building my list," she says. "So I'm very accustomed to working with writers who are relatively new to the industry. I think Clara and I shared a real sense of excitement and wonderment at the whole process."

Clara and Stacy signed together and started working on the project. The proposal sold fairly quickly, but that was just the beginning. Clara had a lot to learn about writing, and she had to work under a tight deadline. She credits Stacy with talking her down from numerous literary ledges.

Stacy says that much of her work with Clara and other debut writers involves coaching them not to get too far ahead of themselves, something first-time authors have a tendency to do. She says that many writers, Clara included, worry too much about something that's two or ten steps down the line, so Stacy helps them focus on the immediate tasks in front of them. Clara is grateful for the entire whirlwind process, and Stacy's role in it, and while she acknowledges that most writers won't be able replicate her experience, she's sure that some of it can be useful. She points out that having a clear sense of what she wanted from the beginning helped her make the right decisions down the line.

Out of the Slush Pile

Agents jumped into Clara Bensen's inbox before she ever considered writing a book, whereas Delilah Dawson admits she might have jumped into agent's inboxes a little too early. But she doesn't regret it — in fact, she advocates it for others.

The origins of the term *slush pile* are debated[1] — it might come from the task of sifting through rotting vegetation or pans of gold, or from the frequent references to "slush" as nonsense by nineteenth-century writers, or from the slush funds distributed by ship officers. No matter where the term originated, it has shady undertones and origins, and now squarely refers to the drudgery of going through swaths of unread manuscripts submitted to agents and editors.

No one seems to look forward to their slush piles. One agent even created a humor site called *Slush Pile Hell*, dedicated to poorly written submissions. But for many aspiring writers without established connections or previous publications, the slush pile is also the place where they find themselves when they're seeking representation.

Delilah's take on the whole query process was to jump in at the deep end and see where it took her. She wrote the first draft of her first book in the summer of 2009, and by that fall she had started querying agents. "That tells you a lot right there," she says. "I hear people advise, 'Don't query too soon,' but I'm of the opinion that everyone queries too soon. You might as well dive right into it fearlessly and learn from it. You're going to learn a lot more from fifty rejected queries than you would from sitting at home twiddling your thumbs."

Besides, she argues, no matter who you are or how accomplished your work is, publishing doesn't move fast. So beyond learning from the process, she knew that the earlier she started, the quicker that ball would start rolling. She says authors should push themselves outside their comfort zone, not wait for a magical day when they feel fully prepared and doubt free — that day will never come. At the same time, she recognizes that some people pursue publication for the wrong reasons. As much as she advocates getting your work out, she says it should always be about the writer's internal wants rather than any external shoulds.

Delilah thinks most new writers have an artificial sense of a clock ticking down. Before she queried, she frequently worried about someone else writing her book, taking all her brilliant ideas, and querying before she did. With many books now behind her, she doesn't believe that anymore. There are many different ways to build even similar storylines, and the best approach is to write your best book, then find it a home. "Query when you want to, not because you think you need to. A great book will always find its place, whether you query today or far down the road."

Delilah received a number of rejections, and she worked through them, revising the structure of her query, the shape of her first chapter, and her approach to reaching out to agents. When she started to receive some interest from agents, including requests for partial or full manuscripts, she responded. She eagerly awaited their responses but still faced generic rejection. Finally, after many more attempts and another request to see her manuscript, she received a more personal response. Agents Joanna Stampfel-Volpe and Jim McCarthy, whom Delilah thanks in her acknowledgments, both reached out. In different ways, they told her that she had talent and writing chops, but they also told her the book she was querying was dead on arrival. It didn't fit some of the rules of the romance genre — for example, one of her main characters committed infidelity. They both asked her to keep each of them in mind if she wrote something else.

Delilah dusted herself off and looked at her query and manuscript. It was the first time she had something more concrete to go on than general rejection. She had also started reaching out about some of the other manuscripts she was working on, including a middle-grade book. It was that middle-grade query, for a book that has never been published, that drew the attention from two agents. They both requested full manuscripts. In a strange twist, Delilah says, "after six months and more than 130 rejections, I received two offers of representation on the same day."

She spoke with each agent, and ultimately decided to work with Kate McKean because they connected well and she thought Kate could represent the full breadth of her work. Both of them acknowledge that Delilah's early work needed more seasoning and development, but Kate explains that sometimes an agent needs to see past that and identify a writer with promise. "What I found in Delilah's work early on was its ability to make me forget I was reading a submission. It drew me in, kept me turning pages, and called to me to come back when I wasn't reading it. Even if things are rough around the edges in a submission, if those qualities are on the page, I'll likely want to talk to the author more. Of course, writers looking for representation can't know what it is about their books that will produce that response in an agent—and every agent reacts differently to submissions. But the things a writer can control are a focus on a plot with movement and real stakes, characters who are fleshed out and believable, and attention to prose that shows the author has edited the work as much as they can.

"That last part is the key element to differentiating the 'needing some work' writers from the 'too lazy to edit themselves' writers," she continues. "A writer won't know how a line will land with a particular reader, but a good writer will understand how to take out clunky sentences, unnecessary description, typos, grammatical errors, clichés, passive voice, and general flabbiness. I'm looking for writers who already know how to kill their darlings, so I won't have to. It takes some practice, but all writers can become better self-editors. When I find those writers who just 'need a little work,' they've all done everything they can to self-edit before I even get my hands on it."

Kate and Delilah started working together on the middle-grade manuscript, but even after many rounds of edits and submissions, it would never find a home. That led them to talk about other projects Delilah was working on. She told Kate about the first book in what would become the Blud series, and when they agreed to abandon the middle-grade book, they focused their attention on *Wicked as They Come*.

That shift was difficult for Delilah. Some part of her acknowledges that she believed that once you got an agent, especially one of Kate McKean's reputation, you were set and it was just a matter of time before your book sold. At auction. With fancy parties to follow.

Now with multiple publications behind her, Delilah still faces rejection all the time, and she realizes it's just part of the writing life no matter how much success you find. But it took her a while to adjust her thinking, and it's something she thinks other writers can learn from. Having an agent helps, but you will still see more than what you think is your fair share of rejection, she says. As Delilah faced another round of rejection, she asked herself a question that many of the authors profiled for this book echoed when they discussed setbacks: why did she want this? If she stripped away all the other aspects of her writing life, she recognized that at her core, she wanted this book to come out because she had loved writing it.

Even today, when times get tough, she continues to remind herself of that feeling. "I'll have times where I get really worried about my career or living up to my own expectations, and I have to remind myself, 'You can quit this today. You don't actually need to do this.' This is fun, and when it's fun, I feel like you're more free to make interesting choices."

Though they write in different genres and styles, Rebecca Makkai and Cynthia Bond also found their agent, Nicole Aragi, through the slush-pile query process. But even with a similar process, they took different paths from Delilah and each other.

Nicole Aragi is one of the most respected agents in publishing, with a list of clients that includes Jonathan Safran Foer, Edwidge Danticat, Colson Whitehead, and Junot Díaz. Cynthia Bond's mentors and friends told her that Nicole would be a great fit for her work.

So she researched her and decided to query, but not in the typical way. "Everyone told me that to get an agent, you write a query letter, wait, send them work, wait, and then wait some more. I said to myself, 'I'm not going to do that,' so I just decided to start calling people."

She found the number for Nicole's office and called and left this message: "Hi, my name is Cynthia. I wrote a novel. When I was a child, I sat on Maya Angelou's lap. Call me back." Perhaps not surprisingly, she didn't hear back. So she reverted to the standard query process, reaching out to several other agents.

Months later, she started to receive some attention from a few other agents, but she still couldn't shake the idea that she wanted to work with Nicole. So she called Nicole's office back, "as if I'd never called before," and this time they invited her to submit a query. Soon after, Nicole reached out to Cynthia to request a full manuscript, and some weeks later she called to say she loved her book and wanted to represent her. "I got off the phone and I screamed like I'd won the lottery. My daughter was really young, and she came running in and thought I'd been hurt."

Years before Rebecca Makkai and Nicole Aragi worked together, Rebecca remembers writing Nicole's name on a piece of scrap paper. She wasn't close to finishing her manuscript, but she was doing some agent research. Nicole was her first choice, even if her list of superstar authors was daunting. "It was sort of like a thirteen-year-old boy seeing a poster of Christie Brinkley and saying, 'That's going to be my girlfriend.' So I just wrote her name down and it stayed there on my desk for more than three years."

Those three years later, Rebecca began to receive positive responses from other agents, including the one who suggested she revisit *The Borrower*. Around the same time, she was cleaning her desk and found that piece of paper with Nicole's name on it. "And I just felt like if I didn't try it, I'd regret it. I also felt so sure she'd say no that once she did, I could move on to more realistic expectations. When I was twenty-one, I sent a story to the *New Yorker*, which is hilarious. There was one percent of me that was delusional, but 99 percent of me wanted it to be my first rejection. And I felt the same way about querying Nicole."

To Rebecca's surprise, Nicole wrote her back and told her that she was headed on a two-week vacation but that she was halfway through the book and couldn't stop thinking about it. When Rebecca replied to thank her, she received Nicole's "out of the office" message, which said she'd return on August 28. "I'd somehow convinced myself that she'd write me back on August 29, as if she's not the busiest person in the world."

A week into September, Rebecca lost her nerve. She wanted to check in with Nicole, but she didn't want to seem like an overly anxious writer. "So I had this fake email account, as many of us do to sign up for a free something or other, and I wanted to see if I'd still get an 'out of office' message. But I didn't know what to say, so somehow I decided that the appropriate thing to do was to write her a spam message. So the subject line read something like 'Increase Your Manhood With These New Pills' and the email linked to some Viagra website."

Rebecca sent it and didn't get an out-of-office reply, which spooked her even more. Nicole was back, and her mind started racing with imagined reasons that Nicole hadn't written her back yet. "Oh no, it falls apart. She must hate the ending. It's so bad that she's too nervous to even tell me."

But after simmering on those doubts for a couple of days, Rebecca received an email from Nicole asking to set up a phone call, and they started working together soon after. Rebecca says she's still pretty sure Nicole Aragi doesn't know that she spammed her.

Publishing Work First

One of the things Rebecca had going for her when she queried Nicole was that by then she'd already been featured in *Best American Short Stories* several years in a row. Although she took the query route, those publication credits likely helped her in the query process. Two of the authors profiled for this book didn't even need to query; they were approached because of work they'd already published.

Alan Heathcock has worked with two separate agents in his career, and they both started working with him based on his short fiction. Alan worked with his first agent after he published a story in the *Harvard Review*. They worked together for a while, but eventually they both thought it was time for a change. In 2005 Alan published "Peacekeeper" in the *Virginia Quarterly Review*. That story was then selected for inclusion in the 2006 edition of *Best American Mystery Stories*.

Though it was a big break, Alan worried that it might corner him into being a mystery writer. "As proud as I was of that, I felt like I couldn't tell some people." He had a fear that others might think less of him, like he was supposed to aspire to be included only in *Best American Short Stories*. "I've always felt that any genre can be deeply literary. My crime stories were getting at something deeper than the crimes themselves. But in graduate programs, I felt a push-back against it, so I carried that with me even after it came out.

"Now that I've passed through it all, I embrace it all. But I think there are great misunderstandings within whatever genre corners you find yourself. We would have better writers coming out of MFA programs if we all just declared that we can still have deep and important conversations if they're about plot."

As Alan worried about the implications of being included in the mystery anthology, Sarah Burnes at the Gernert Company reached out to him and asked if he was seeking agent representation. Soon after, they started working together. She found Alan through his anthologized story, but contrary to his fears, she never saw him as solely a crime or mystery writer, and "Peacekeeper" would become one of the anchor stories in Alan's collection *Volt*.

"With Sarah I found someone who not only liked my work but also understood me as a writer," says Alan. "She got me, she understood what I was trying to do. She liked that I was writing heavy stories, and she liked that they were short stories, which is not always the case. And most of all, she expressed a vision for what my career might look like and how she could help me. And I just found a kindred spirit, someone who could help me on the business side of things. She's very good at what she does."

Courtney Maum's agent, Rebecca Gradinger, also found her through her short stories. Courtney had published some work with online publications, which led a few agents to reach out to her. Rebecca was one of them, but as fate would have it, her message somehow got lost in an email filter. Courtney didn't read the message from Rebecca for about a year, and by that time she'd already started working with another agent—her second agent at the time.

But Courtney and her existing agent weren't quite seeing eye to eye. Around that time Courtney, while searching through her Facebook messages for something else entirely, found a bunch of unread messages. One of them was from Rebecca Gradinger, asking if she'd ever like to talk about her work.

Courtney is good friends with the novelist Maggie Shipstead, who is also represented by Rebecca. She'd heard Maggie talk about how great her agent was, so she decided to respond to the message, almost a year after it was sent. They set up a time to talk. Meanwhile Courtney reached out to Maggie, who told her, "'You'll never have a better agent than Rebecca.' And, well, I tend to listen to whatever Maggie says because she's a very level-headed person."

So they met and talked about Courtney's work, and connected well, but more important to Courtney, they also talked about things beyond her work. They discussed the direction of her writing career and how the relationships with previous agents had gone astray and, most of all, how Courtney wanted to find an agent she could partner with to move her career forward, not just a single project. "Before Rebecca, I thought you just picked an agent that you could be friends with, someone you could pal around with and talk about literature with, and it took me two agents like that to realize that no, you want to connect, but you want a business partner more."

Building Relationships

If agents didn't find them and they didn't query, then how did the rest of the authors find representation? Through chance and connections.

In addition to *Inked*, Eric Smith is the author of *The Geek's Guide to Dating*, published by Quirk Books, where Eric worked at the time. The publisher, Jason Rekulak, had approached Eric with the idea for the guide. "I'd been writing about geek culture for a while and had been talking about a new girl I was dating," says Eric. "So he asked me if I could combine those interests."

When Eric started to pull together *The Geek's Guide to Dating*, he'd already been long at work on his young adult novel. In fact, he finished the *Inked* manuscript well before *The Geek's Guide to Dating*, and while he was working on the guide, he reached out to agent Dawn Frederick of Red Sofa Literary after meeting one of her colleagues, Jennie Goloboy, in the Quirk Books office. He was able to lead off his query letter to Dawn with a personal touch because of that connection:

> *Eric from Quirk Books here. As you've seen on my personal blog and Twitter (thanks for reading and following!), I dabble in writing when I'm not busy promoting other people's books. And I wanted to pitch you my book first because, well, I've seen what a fantastic job you've done with Stacey Graham. Sending Jennie to our office to actually meet us? I've been here almost two years, and I've never seen that kind of personal attention from a literary agent. I still talk about that! It's the sort of close attention I try to give all the authors I work with, and it's what I'd love from an agent.*

Dawn responded right away. And in what may be the most fortunate of all these author stories, Eric Smith began 2012 with a book deal and a new agent without ever receiving a single rejection.

Brian Benson didn't face rejection either when he looked for an agent. His year-long Atheneum program through the Attic in Portland was halfway complete, and at the halfway point you switch mentors. He'd been working with the author Karen Karbo, and one day she pulled him aside and told him she really liked what he was working on, and when he completed the program maybe they could talk further. "That was pretty much the best day of my life as a writer. The idea that this wonderful writer, who'd published a bunch of books, liked my work was very validating."

So after Brian completed the program, now working with Cheryl Strayed, he wrote Karen. He was hoping she'd give him some tips on finding an agent. But he didn't hear back right away and left for a family trip to Sweden. During the trip his backpack was stolen with his laptop in it, including three unsaved chapters. "The first rule of writing, kids," says Brian: "Back up your work, back up your work!"

But two days after his laptop was stolen, Karen wrote him to say, "Great news. I talked to my agent, David Forrer, and he'd like to see your work—are you ready to send it?" Brian was only expecting Karen to give him some pointers or advice, not to make the formal introduction and connection to her agent. "I was thinking I would take some baby steps," says Brian. "But Karen just kind of shoved me into the pool, and I'm grateful she did."

But now he had to rewrite those three missing chapters from *Going Somewhere*, and quickly. So he contacted David, explained the situation, and asked if he could get back to him in a month with the missing portion of his manuscript. "A month later, I sent him about half the book, and we signed soon after. The only agent I ever contacted."

Edan Lepucki's good friend Emma Straub helped her connect with her agent, Erin Hosier. At the time, as noted earlier, Edan's first agent had dropped her. Emma had worked with Erin Hosier on an early work that never sold, and although they weren't working together anymore, they had remained close. Emma thought Edan's first book would be perfect for Erin Hosier, so she connected the two of them.

Edan sent Erin her still unsold manuscript for *The Book of Deeds* and didn't hear back for months. Edan was pretty sure it wouldn't lead anywhere, but as with many of our other authors, it just took time. Erin reached out to Edan months later and said she wanted to represent her. She said she would soon be in Los Angeles, Edan's hometown, and wondered if they could meet up. Edan went to the meeting thinking they'd talk about how to sell the work, but Erin arrived and said, "I'm sorry to say it, but this book isn't going to sell."

Edan remembers feeling a little taken back. "But I thought you liked it," she replied. So Erin told Edan that she loved her work, and that she was going to help her send out this book, but that it won't sell. She said that she wanted to work with her over the long haul, that she loved her short stories and her voice, and that she just needed to find the right story. So Edan told her about her close-to-finished *California* manuscript, and Erin told her it sounded interesting and to keep working on it.

Erin did shop Edan's first book around, and she was right, it didn't sell. But Edan really valued Erin's honesty and her long-term vision. "It felt really different for someone to say to me, 'I believe in you and your voice and your vision, and I'm taking you on as a client even though I have questions about your salability in the short term.' That was really important to me. It made me feel like she'll stick with me through all of my work, even if everything isn't a commercial success."

The Independent Path

And what about the choice to self-publish? A number of our authors either explored or chose that option. When it came to Delilah Dawson's first book, she had no doubts about her preferred approach. "I do not have the skills or the self-selling expertise to be a purely self-published author. I knew that from the start. What I really wanted to do was write the books and to let other more competent people — with enthusiasm and knowledge — handle those other aspects of it."

Most of Delilah's books have been traditionally published, but she has also made the decision to self-publish some of her work, enough that she would be described as a hybrid author. She has self-published several erotica books under a pen name. And she joined writers Chuck Wendig and Kevin Hearne to self-publish a short novella by each in a book called *Three Slices.*

Delilah says she is agnostic when it comes to her publishing decisions. She values traditional publishing most of the time, but sometimes self-publishing just makes more sense. At the Romance Writers of America conference in 2013, she heard agent Kristin Nelson of Nelson Literary Agency talk about hybrid authors, or authors who were traditionally publishing and self-publishing. "She had run the numbers, and on the whole, hybrid authors made 15 percent more than their counterparts. And I was like 'Awesome, I'll take that.'"

Now Delilah weighs her projects carefully, deciding which make sense for a traditional publisher and which are better released through her own legwork. Most of the decisions tie into questions of audience, platform, and timing. If she has a built-in audience or the timing is more critical, she'll experiment with self-publishing the work, but for her major titles, especially the ones developed in a series, she continues to want to work with a traditional publisher.

Edan Lepucki seemed to be in a place where self-publishing could have made sense. Her first agent had dropped her, and her novel manuscript had been rejected at multiple turns. She researched her options, and as she considered it, she became certain that she didn't want to pursue self-publishing. In wrestling with that decision, she wrote an essay for *The Millions* titled "Reasons Not to Self Publish"[2] —it has been frequently shared.

Since the time of that essay, she admits that she has met stellar self-published authors who have taken control of their process and found an audience. But in Edan's experience, self-published authors far too often employ overly aggressive, sometimes desperate, marketing tactics. She says those authors give a bad name to the really good self-publishing authors. Edan knew she didn't want to be in that position, especially for her first book.

"I'm not really an early adopter of anything," says Edan. "So I didn't want to be the guinea pig to set out. And I also knew I wanted a really good editor; I wanted someone to do the publicity, even if I'm doing most of the legwork; I wanted people with lots of experience guiding my way."

She also says that it's not a good idea to rush to publish. She thinks her abandoned manuscript is best left abandoned. If she had hastily self-published it, her first book would have been less strong than *California* was. "*California* was ultimately a much better book, and having it be my first book was much better for my career in the long run," says Edan.

For Monona Wali, the decision to self-publish came after trying to pursue traditional publishing for her manuscript. She didn't come to the decision lightly, but she felt like she'd reached a dead end for her manuscript, and if it was ever going to exist in the world, she needed to do it herself. She'd also seen some of the aforementioned aggressive authors and questionable tactics in the self-publishing world, and she struggled through the stigma even as she decided to pursue the option.

Monona started with an agent. She worked with her and sent out *My Blue Skin Lover* through several rounds to publishers. It would go out, the two of them would get a little feedback in rejection, and Monona would work on revising it before they sent it out again. This cycle continued, with some positive feedback but never anything that led to a sale.

As the discouraging responses piled up, Monona and her agent started to drift apart. That was hard, she says. The more her book was rejected, the more it seemed her agent was losing interest in the project, and after many months without word from any publishers, Monona felt like her agent had given up. She felt that she needed to move on, but she dreaded going through the agent search all over again. So she began to approach small presses on her own, and one press strongly considered publishing the book. The press had her manuscript for close to a year before sending her a rejection. "And then I kind of just gave up on it," says Monona. "So it sat on my shelf for about two years. I just didn't know what to do with it. Self-publishing was so new, and it just had such a stigma about it, so I never really considered it."

It might have sat on the shelf forever, but Monona also teaches creative writing at Santa Monica College and she had a student with a lot of marketing experience. He studied closely with her while working on his own memoir, and she told him a bit about her abandoned book. She remembers distinctly what he said to her: "What are you doing about it? What are you going to do, just let it sit there? Just fucking publish it."

Monona says the way he spoke, making it sound so simple and defiant, had a big impact on her. She had never even considered taking control of the process. She had always pictured it as a traditionally published book, and she didn't know anything about self-publication. She walked away from that interaction asking herself, "'He's right—what am I doing here?' I still believed in the book, and I just said, 'What do I have to lose?' So that was the impulse." A later chapter will discuss the steps Monona took to self-publish, but it was the conversation with her student that put her on the path to having her book out in the world.

Zetta Elliott came to her decision to pursue self-publishing after her experiences with traditionally publishing her debut book, *Bird*. In 2005 *Bird* won the Lee & Low New Voices contest, which came with a cash award and the potential for a publishing contract. As noted earlier, however, Zetta was asked to "age up" her manuscript from picture book to young adult, which ran counter to every impulse she had in writing it.

It was at this time that the illustrator Shadra Strickland read Zetta's manuscript. She loved it and started working on a set of illustrations to accompany the text. "If Shadra hadn't read the manuscript and fallen in love with it, and done a full set of sketches for the book so that they could see what this book might look like, I don't know if I would have this book to this day."

Bird did publish traditionally, and it won numerous awards and found critical praise. Still, its path to publication didn't sit well with

Zetta. "People don't often want to engage with the fact that the relationship between an editor and a writer is so much about power. And so you have marginalized writers stepping into the publishing arena, where they are further marginalized. There's nobody black working at a particular publishing house, and so somebody white is telling a black author, 'I don't think we can sell this unless you change it or tone it down a bit.'"

Zetta explains that this situation dates back to slave narratives. When fugitive slaves wrote about their experiences, the narratives always began with somebody "white and respectable who would write a preface saying, 'I know this negro and she is honest.' If you trace publishing since those narratives, some of those same dynamics still exist."

Zetta didn't want to go through this for her future work. She wanted control. She wants other writers of color to have that control too. Luckily, at the time, self-publishing was growing as a real option. Just a few years after *Bird* was published, it was even more accessible, and Zetta is now helping other writers of color who want to follow in her footsteps. "I'm starting to teach workshops on this because it's so frustrating to me that so many people have been told their whole lives that they don't have a story worth sharing, and they've all started to believe it."

Zetta hasn't entirely abandoned the traditional publishing path. She did publish a children's picture book, *Melena's Jubilee*, in 2016 with Tilbury House. In fact, she now splits her projects into books that she thinks might have a shot at being traditionally published and ones she doesn't think have a prayer. "Certain books have more explicit political messages," she says. "If I want to talk about Black Lives Matter, a lynching, or the refugee crisis, I'm not going to water it down. So for the traditional publishing, I tend to pick the books that most editors would find universal."

What would Zetta do if she were a still-aspiring writer of color? She recommends thinking about your work, what it is, and what ideas you want to present to the world. If it's a fit for the traditional publishing world, then go for that, but if it isn't, don't change it and don't give up. "I haven't given up entirely on the traditional publishing industry, but the institutional and structural problems are so deep that it's hard. I've fought through and gone around all the obstacles, but I'm sure there are hundreds and hundreds of writers of color who have just given up."

Ruby author Cynthia Bond, a writer of color herself, doesn't disagree that the deck is stacked against writers of color. She knows a number of very talented people who have gone down the self-publishing path, but the traditional path is still the one she advocates as the first option. She believes it's still the way to get the most people to read your book.

"Is it more difficult? Of course it is. If you're black and female, it's even tougher. Everything is incredibly racist and sexist everywhere you go, and publishing is no different, but I'm going to keep going. I'm sure there are authors who are too radical or too experimental or too outside the parameters of what a publisher is looking for, and each author has to decide their own personal destiny, but I do also think that writers of color should knock on those doors first. It would be a shame if they didn't just because they heard it was impossible."

In the end, the path to publication is full of possibility and room to experiment. With so many different approaches to representation and publication, there isn't one right path anymore, and the common theme between these authors seems to be that they had a vision, did their research, and stayed patient until they found the right fit. Even after they pursued a path, if it didn't succeed they were open to other options.

The Publishing Decision

There are more routes to publishing your book all the time, and choosing one can be a daunting and confusing decision. Several of the authors profiled for this book have moved into a hybrid method of publishing, working with traditional publishers when it makes sense and tackling self-published projects at other times. But even if you might someday pursue different methods, you do need to make a decision for your current project. Here are four major questions to help you make the publishing decision for your first book.

What Is My Purpose in Publishing?

As a first step, get honest and ask yourself some tough questions. Am I willing to go through months and even years of rejection to pursue the traditionally published path? How much do I care about the prestige of the imprint, or whether my book has more potential to be reviewed in prestigious places or sold in bookstores or win awards? When it comes down to it, am I doing this because I want my book out in the world, or do I want something more out of the publishing experience?

Maybe the best way to answer these questions is to picture your finished book. Whether it's an e-book only or published in multiple formats, ask yourself what it looks like in your mind's eye. If you can stick with that vision, the rest of the decisions will fall into line.

What Genre Am I Writing In, and
Where Do Most Readers Seek Out That Genre?

Sometimes it pays to be a trailblazer, but bucking market trends will make the publishing journey that much more difficult. The most lucrative genre for self-publishing is romance because of the purchasing patterns of readers. There are other niches where self-publishing is less likely to succeed. Do your research, find titles similar to your book, and find out how they were published.

This is not to say that you can't forge your own path. Someone always has to start a new trend. But if you are going against market trends, you need to ask yourself how much you're up for that challenge in an already very challenging business.

What Roadblocks Are in My Way, and
What Options Best Allow Me to Overcome Them?

Authors decide to self-publish for a number of reasons, more than this chapter can cover. But in many cases the decision comes down to reducing barriers. When a book can't find a publisher, it can mean the story needs more work, but it may actually have nothing to do with the quality of the writing.

Good stories sometimes simply cannot find a publisher. The barrier could be market trends, marginalization or systemic exclusion, author platform, or upcoming needs of the publisher. Some authors will decide to wait those barriers out or keep trying, others will abandon the project and move on to something else, while still others will decide that the book deserves to see the light of day and publish it themselves.

How Much Control Do I Want over My Project?
How Much of the Business Side Can I Take On?

Self-publishing gives you total control, but it also gives you the complete burden. Some authors love the idea of doing it themselves, building an audience, and forming an independent solo business. Others begrudge the work of publicity, the networking, the self-promotion, and really want to focus on just the storytelling and writing. It's also possible to hire help for things like cover design or publicity even when you self-publish, which muddies the water even more.

Again, there's no right answer, but it is important to figure out your comfort level with all facets of publishing a book and to make your publishing decisions fit your interests and willingness.

8. Setbacks and Perseverance

Doubt, delay, and distraction are the shipwrecking crags in the author's journey to publication. Authors must find a way to avoid them in the face of setback and rejection. Every writer profiled for this book told stories of setback. Even the few whose initial efforts found charmed, rejectionless paths eventually came upon barriers to completing and publishing their work.

With all the obstacles, it's clear that successful debut authors must possess one important skill that never shows up in book blurbs or Goodreads reviews: perseverance.

It's the most universal part of these authors' stories. Some of our authors even shelved or gave up on their projects for many years, but something brought each of them back. At every step, they could come upon new reasons to doubt their project, their prospects, or their own skills. As we'll see, the ability to overcome those doubts was less about self-assurance and more about determination when confidence lapsed.

Setbacks while Writing

For most, setbacks and challenges first presented themselves within the writing itself. Clara Bensen essentially plunged into a crash course in authorship, with little time to learn her craft. At the time she signed her book contract, she'd never written anything longer than a forty-page college paper. "I knew there was a story to tell, so I never doubted that part, but I did wonder, 'Do I have the experience and skill to pull this off in a way that I'm going to be proud of?'"

Without any mentorship, writing community, or publishing knowledge — things that she has worked hard to develop in the time since — she had no choice but to jump in on her own. She says she moved forward by treating the whole writing process much as she treated her cross-globe trip — as an experiment to see where it would all lead.

But even with that open mindset, doubt and anxiety crept in. Enough that she refused to show her work to anyone, including her agent, Stacy Testa. She felt an extra guilt in that refusal because of the book's subject matter. "I'm writing this book about letting go and dealing with anxiety, and the entire time I'm writing, I'm having panic attacks. It all sounds so perfect, but there are many drawbacks to going viral and getting swept up by agents and all that because it wasn't like I'd built up a writing career or support system over time; I was just thrown into it."

Clara did consider asking for new deadlines or trying to stop altogether and pay back her advance, but when it came down to it, she wanted this book to come out. She believed she had a meaningful story to tell and that she was the only one who could tell it. "I just had to keep telling myself that I'm doing the best that I can do. I'm as good as I am, and there's no way I can speed up that process."

Clara had a contract and a deadline to drive her; in the absence of those two pressures, doubt was an even stronger force for some of the other authors. Since *The Borrower* took many years to write, Rebecca Makkai's writing career developed as she wrote it. By the time the book came out, she'd published short stores in prestigious publications and received a number of accolades for them. But until those things started happening, she felt sheepish about going off to write. "When I first started writing *The Borrower*, I hadn't published anything. So I'd feel really silly taking off writing on a Saturday, telling my husband, 'I'm really sorry, I'll be back in six hours.' He was always very supportive, but until you're published, you have that impostor syndrome, and it feels more like an indulgence or silly hobby."

Self-doubt sometimes also creeps in because of what others tell you to do. Before Courtney Maum abandoned her original manuscript, her first agent shopped the book around but it wasn't selling. She remembers that agent saying, "We can't keep sending your book out, so can you write a memoir about your time in Paris instead?"

Courtney now knows that was the moment she needed to change agents, but at the time she didn't have the experience or confidence to think that way. After many rejections, she says, "when someone finally pays attention to your writing, you grab onto them. So it never occurred to me to say no, and I started to write the memoir."

She says she wasted a lot of time with a memoir she never had an interest in writing. Courtney had asked to see all her rejection letters from editors. Many of the letters said they loved the writing but the character wasn't sympathetic enough and therefore the book wouldn't be commercial enough. So when Courtney turned to the suggested memoir, she said to herself, "I'm going to write a commercial book." That thought began a spiral for her. "I started overwriting what I thought would sell, which is absolutely the way to guarantee that you're not going to sell anything. I wrote two books that year; they're both really bad."

Abandoning the Work

One of the greatest setbacks a writer can face is to abandon a project and move on. It often represents letting go of years of work, perhaps just as well spent with frozen drinks on a beach.

As we've seen, Alan Heathcock spent three years writing two novel manuscripts, but at a certain point he needed to let them go. "It was crushing," he says. "But the one thing I've found as an artist is that you have to be clear-eyed. You can't try to pretend that you have something when you don't. In hindsight, I'm now very proud of the younger version of me, who was able to say 'This is not working' and then moved on to the next thing." Years and a lot more hard work were required for Alan to turn his material into the esteemed collection we now know as *Volt*.

Similarly, Edan Lepucki had to abandon her first novel manuscript. Edan had intended to spend her time in her UCross residency working with her agent's notes to revise the manuscript — but her agent dropped her just before she headed to UCross. It was very difficult for her to refocus her plans in the short time before she left for the residency. Yet she gathered herself and turned her attention to starting *California*.

But Edan hadn't fully let go of her first manuscript. A few months after returning from the residency, Edan found her current agent, Erin Hosier. Erin liked the writing in Edan's first manuscript, but she didn't think it would sell. They began to work together regardless, and Erin proved to be right. Edan had to face the reality that her manuscript just wasn't ready, so she had to find the resilience to move on and focus on *California*. It wasn't easy. "Everybody has that moment when they say, 'I'm horrible,'" she says.

In the end, her experience with her first novel helped her next project. "*California* was much easier to write. With my first novel, I'd never tried to write one before, and I learned so much about novel writing from that process. I kept asking myself, 'What should happen now?,' and it felt patched together. *California* was definitely difficult to write at times, but it felt right from the beginning. I felt in my bones that it would get published."

Delilah Dawson had to abandon a middle-grade book about a little girl with goblins, talking rats, and a haunted attic. She and her agent, Kate McKean, worked on it together and tried to sell it. She recalls that many publishers liked parts of it, but ultimately after many months and multiple rejections, she and Kate agreed it wasn't going to sell.

Letting go of that manuscript hurt. She thought the concept was really fun, and she says she'd always looked forward to seeing it on a bookshelf somewhere. Now five or more years later, she's grateful it wasn't her debut book. "I read it recently and I know why it didn't sell now. I apparently had not met a ten-year-old in the prior thirty years. The kid just moves around the story like a Lego block, and the story is very flat. Looking back, I'm really glad I didn't try to self-publish it, because even though I now also see some faults in *Wicked as They Come*, I'm glad it was my debut book."

And sometimes abandonment is only temporary. As we've seen, Monona Wali, Courtney Maum, and Rebecca Makkai all returned to their manuscripts after significant stretches of time. When they left them behind, they did not intend to return. They turned to other projects or moved forward with other kinds of work, and thought of that first manuscript as just for practice. As Rebecca puts it, "I thought it was just for me. A totally flawed work not worth rescuing."

Dealing with Rejection

Doubt usually happens internally first, but writers also get to experience it from external forces. There are multiple junctions where a writer faces rejection—from peers in a critique or writing group, from agents through a query, or from publishers not wanting to publish the work.

A few of our authors had worked as professional editors. For Alan Heathcock, that dual role lent him an even more humbling set of doubts. He was an editor at the literary magazine *Mid-American Review*, and he'd started to send out his own work to literary magazines and get rejections. But the kicker for him was rejecting other people's stories that "were better than the stories I was sending out. That was deeply humbling."

It led to bit of a crisis: he recalls some long nights with little sleep wondering if he was cut out for the writing life. But he never really considered quitting. Being rejected while reading stronger stories that still had to be rejected pushed him even more. "I'd just keep asking myself, 'How do I get to the next plateau?'"

He tinkered, and read, and reworked, and revised. He says that after that experience, even now, when he revises a story and thinks it is publishable, that's not the moment he sends it out. He no longer asks himself if it's publishable; he asks if he can make it any better. Only when he can honestly answer no to that question does he send it out.

A rejection of his story "Peacekeeper" helped him firm up this approach. He'd submitted the story to a few places, including the *Atlantic*. He knew it was a good story. He got a handwritten note from the *Atlantic* editor, who admired the writing but also said, "Your sequencing and chronology doesn't seem to be working as well as it could be." Alan reread the story with fresh eyes and agreed. In fact, he acknowledged that he had already known it but had sent the story out anyway.

The next time he submitted the revised story, the *Virginia Quarterly Review* published it, and it went on to win awards and be anthologized.

He says that writers who don't learn from rejection are missing part of the point. "I think about that story all the time. I knew it could be improved before I sent it out the first time, but I sent it out nonetheless. And if I had let my ego get in the way, and took that rejection slip and said, 'Well, screw you, what do you know?,' it wouldn't have got to the place where it finally got to go."

And yet there's a big difference between letting go of ego to create your best work and changing work you believe in because of frequent rejection. As noted earlier, rejection only fueled Zetta Elliott's resolve. When she first started submitting *Bird*, before she'd won the Lee & Low Prize for it, she was hearing back from people that it was just too sad for a children's picture book. "Yes, it is sad, but that's not the point. There are so many kids who are dealing with this experience."

Around the time she first started hearing this feedback, some of her academic research led her to the Cooperative Children's Book Center at the University of Wisconsin. Each year it publishes well-researched and dire statistics regarding how few people of color succeed in publishing children's literature. "It was just horrifying to see. Sometimes it's easy for people to say, 'Oh, just try harder and stay positive.' But the numbers showed it wasn't anything about the individual or attitude; there was institutional racism at play."

She started to realize how that related to the feedback she was receiving about *Bird*. "So you have white women editors feeling like this book is too tragic or that it needs to be written for older kids or that it crystallizes stereotypes about the black experience. As I learned more, all of that started to feel racialized to me."

The combination of her own experience and the research she was seeing forced Zetta to ask some significant questions about her work. Should she soften it? Should she write it for a different age group to ensure that it would get published? She briefly considered these options, but in talking to friends and other writers, she realized how strongly she felt. These points were nonnegotiable. "It definitely made me defiant. I was saying you are going to reckon with this narrative whether you like it or not, and I just felt like it deserved to have a place in the world as it was written."

While Zetta needed to find the strength to stick by her work, other authors needed to find the strength to listen and make changes. In a long editorial letter to Delilah Dawson about *Wicked as They Come*, her agent, Kate McKean, told her that she needed to change her main character, Tish, and completely rewrite the first half of the book. The emailed letter came to Delilah while she was at a restaurant, and she started crying. "I was crying so hard that the cook saw me out the window and brought me a plate of beignets and backed away like he was leaving an antelope carcass for a lion."

Now, many books later, Delilah still has a similar reaction to editorial letters. She equates it to going through the stages of grief. First is anger. "I say 'screw it!' and flip the table and walk away. Then I forget about it for a while, and when I come back I go through grief and depression and acceptance. I never tell anyone that I'm feeling that or send off a hot email, but I'm definitely thinking 'Nope! Not doing that!' But after a while I calm down, and my subconscious starts to figure out how to make all these changes."

Courtney Maum compares rejection to the stages of grief too, and like Delilah, she begins with anger. When the earlier version of *I Am Having So Much Fun Here without You* was rejected, she would dismiss the people who rejected her. She now laughs at what she thought at the time: they were wrong, she didn't want to work with them anyway, they were overlooking a major new voice in fiction. "I was pretty naive back then," she explains.

She's come to learn that rejection and feedback are important parts of her process. "You need to find a balance where you can take the criticism and look at what you're doing, and see where people are right, and still have the confidence in your own work to know when people are wrong. Rejection is all about finding that balance."

Another important lesson Courtney learned is that rejection never stops. Some part of her felt that a publishing deal or a book out in the world might mean less of it. But she says when it came out, she found whole new ways to bring on rejection. "Then the end of the year came, and there are all these Best of the Year book lists. I'd never had to think about that before, and then all of the sudden, with every list I wasn't on, I had all these new ways to be rejected. You just have to be really strong. A lot of really talented people fade away because they can't handle the rejection."

Brian Benson found rejection and criticism even harder in memoir, because he internalized it. After he signed with his agent, David Forrer, and they started to shop *Going Somewhere* around, numerous publishers rejected it before it sold. To write the last bits of the book, Brian had biked back across the country to Wisconsin; he was living with his parents there as the manuscript was being turned down time and again.

"It created so much self-loathing," he says. The rejections wouldn't just come in with a no; each would be accompanied by a spot-on criticism of the manuscript. "Which, being a memoir, also happened to be a spot-on critique of me as a human being. So I'd read things like 'There are many ways in which Benson understands the burdens he places on others, but there are many ways in which he doesn't.'"

Further, remember that Brian had signed on with his agent without receiving any agent rejections, and that he was new to the writing world. Brian says it likely would have been helpful to go through rejection at an earlier stage. When your first rejection isn't about finding an agent or a literary journal, but about your book itself, you can feel unprepared. It started to take its toll. Living with his parents didn't help. After he received some positive interest from a publisher, they told everyone that Brian would soon have a book deal. "So then everyone was asking about it" even though he didn't have a deal, meaning he had to explain himself at every family gathering.

Even once a book comes out, it doesn't relieve the rejection pressure. Cynthia Bond's book launch was just the beginning of the worst period of her writing life. When *Ruby* came out, the *New York Times* had planned to review it, but at the last minute pulled the review, and "that changed the fate of my book." After that review withered, so too did reviews from the *Washington Post* and the *Chicago Tribune*.

Ruby was reviewed in a few places, with glowing praise, but without a review at any of the major venues, the book pretty quickly fell into obscurity. Cynthia had not realized how important those first few weeks were for the viability of her book.

"All of the things that they thought were going to happen for it fell through the floor. My book sales were abysmal, and I lived in terror because I'd only sold the one book. I started to doubt whether the other two in the series would even sell. I also had massive guilt that they'd given me this advance, and every week I'd check the sales and see that *Ruby* was making less and less and less. It was a secret hell that I lived, and I didn't tell anyone."

Of course everything changed when Oprah called, but that's a story for another chapter. Because sometimes the outside pressures just continue to pile up. If you let the outside world pull you down, it can be an immense drag. "Publishing creates this artificial scarcity effect," says Delilah Dawson. "You see everyone else's highlight reel and only your gag reel. You feel like people are constantly writing nineteen books a year, and being on every list, getting starred reviews. Very few people go to Facebook and post, 'I'm sitting at home and haven't bathed in three days and I'm doubting everything I've ever done.' So I feel like those dark periods, those periods of doubt, are even darker because your basis for comparison is flashes of success after success."

Perseverance in the Face of It

Which brings us back to that most important of skills, perseverance. There are so many potential roadblocks, setbacks, and moments of doubt, it seems amazing that anything ever gets published.

"No matter who you are," says Monona Wali, "you're up against a tough reality. I'm a woman of color and an older writer now. The numbers say that the deck is stacked against me. There are success stories, but by and large it's young white men who get published. But no matter who you are, it's tough to make it through."

In the end, she argues, publishing may be a goal but it can't be the purpose. "The thing that always keeps me going is that I love doing this. It's definitely a calling and a passion. And I feel like I have stories to tell that matter to me."

Monona says that in any profession, your mind gets trained to think a certain way. She argues that writers need to train themselves to deal with all the rejection by reminding themselves that they love and believe in the work.

The will to push forward is perhaps best illustrated by Alan Heathcock's first workshop in graduate school. He had grown up in a different world from that of most of his MFA counterparts, and he had read very little at the time he arrived in the program. This fact deeply embarrassed him and drove him. At the first workshop, the class had a two-hour conversation about James Joyce. "I remember walking out, and not only had I not read his books, I had no idea who James Joyce was. I had never heard his name."

So Alan sought out his professor, Wendell Mayo, and asked for his help. He wanted a list of books that he needed to read. Wendell

Mayo gave Alan the list of books he had read for his PhD. "It was a long list that was comprehensive over many periods of literature, starting with *Beowulf* and moving into the modernists," says Alan.

In that first year of graduate school, in addition to all his course and writing work, Alan read 203 books and watched more than 200 movies, examining each for how they told stories. He never again wanted to feel like he had that first day of workshop, so he became deeply invested in learning and growing as a storyteller.

For Zetta Elliott, the question of perseverance is a very straightforward one: she doesn't feel like she has another choice. "If I don't put out these books, they aren't going to exist. If I don't write about a fourteen-year-old black girl with superpowers, it's going to be hard to find that elsewhere."

More to the point, she knows just how significant it is. Like most of the writers profiled for this book, there comes a time when a writer just needs to accept all the roadblocks and barriers and push through them because the story is important, and reaching the reader is the ultimate reward.

"Kids do send me letters," says Zetta. She received a letter with a picture of a young afro-punk black girl. The sides of her head are shaved and she has piercings, just like the girl superhero on the cover of one of Zetta's books. The photo shows the girl holding up Zetta's book with a caption reading, "Finally, a book that looks like me."

"All I need is one message like that, and I'm going to persevere."

Dealing with Setbacks

So how do you deal with all these rejections and setbacks? Here are several tips that came up repeatedly in my interviews with our authors.

Work on Something Else

Side projects or next projects were important to a lot of the writers. It meant they had something to occupy their mind while waiting for responses, and it also meant all their eggs were not in one basket. So if a rejection did come, it wasn't as crushing because it wasn't their one and only project.

If you always have some creative work in the fire, "then whatever you have on submission doesn't matter as much," says Delilah Dawson. "Because as an artist, with any luck, you are now completely in love with this new project."

Steady That Ego

It's hard to read your own work and see it beyond your own perspective. Many of the authors talked about hearing feedback and having to fight the immediate urge to defend your work or to blame the reader. Even if someone radically misread or misunderstood the work, it's far easier to blame the reader than to examine why the reader might have veered off course.

"It's rare to get inside a reader's head," says Cynthia Bond. "Try your best to go with it, instead of fighting it."

Compartmentalize

Rejection is a tough thing, and if you have your connections like phone and email always open while you write, you can ruin your writing sessions. It's best to cordon rejection off until you're ready to deal with it.

Delilah Dawson goes one step further with her agent, Kate McKean: she assigned Kate a specific ringtone on her phone. Per Delilah's request, Kate uses email to send Delilah any bad news or to address logistical issues. She calls only when she has very good news. "So unless I hear that distinctive ring, I'm not expecting good news."

Develop Support

As discussed in chapter 3, a strong writing network and a personal support network can do wonders when the going gets hard. Many of the writers pointed to this as the most important way to deal with everything that gets thrown at you as a writer.

"As you persist and keep pursuing this, you start to develop relationships," says Monona Wali. "Foster those! I have a really great writing community and family support now, and that keeps me going when I need it most."

Remember the Why

Of all the things that got writers through rejection and setback, there was only one universal. Publication, success, and finding readership were all important to the authors, but fundamentally, they all see writing as a way of existing. The process is their purpose. Regardless of how publishing and sales go, they have a passion for writing and they feel compelled to tell their stories.

It's so easy to get caught up in comparisons or doubts, and the profiled authors admit to thinking that way sometimes. But always they pull themselves back by reminding themselves why they do what they do. "I may daydream about best sellers and big awards, but when I'm working, it always comes back to the love of writing and having a story to tell," says Rebecca Makkai.

Buy Some Ice Cream

Sometimes all you can do is try to deal with it the best way you know how. There is a point when you can't make any more changes, when you've considered the work and believe in it, and you just need to find it the right home. Maybe that means changing your scope or publishing choice or outreach, and sometimes it means simply waiting through a process that can sometimes drag and drag.

"Publishing is a slow process, and it takes longer than every author thinks it is going to take," says Eric Smith. "So just be patient. And as for dealing with rejections along the way, well, they're really tough. But feelings are delicious, so I find lots of ice cream works well."

9. Preparing to Publish

After all the setbacks, quandaries, and revisions came the moment all authors hope for: a commitment to publish the book. Many articles and guidebooks cover the stages and mechanics of "getting published," and many authors discuss word counts, book deals, and book launches, yet few ever speak about the quiet and somewhat mysterious period between when a book is sold and when it actually comes out.

But authors do need to consider a number of different issues during this period: publicity, marketing, design, permissions, copyedits, and deadlines. The details vary depending on the type of publisher. It can be a long process with surprising stretches of quiet anxiety, especially for a first-time author who may not be prepared for what's coming.

The Sale

For many of our authors, the sale of their book to a publisher was more anticlimactic than they'd expected. Rebecca Makkai had the good fortune of her manuscript heading to auction with ten editors showing interest. At the time she had a toddler at home, was teaching full time, and was pregnant with her second child. But each of the editors wanted to speak with Rebecca before the auction. "So I'm trying to schedule these ten hour-long phone calls over three days. I'd do one in the morning, go to school, teach for three hours, then while a sub took my class, I'd have a phone call. Then I'd teach three more hours, and then I'd have two or three more phone calls back to back."

She recalls that it felt much more exhausting than exciting. When Rebecca had imagined a manuscript auction, she'd pictured something in between a cattle call and a Sotheby's art sale. But when it all just filtered through her agent's email, the moment didn't really sink in for her. Her manuscript ultimately sold at auction to Viking/Penguin, and her agent, Nicole Aragi, told her afterward how it had all played out. "There wasn't this one moment of excitement. It kind of happened over many long, tiring days, and in retrospect I probably didn't enjoy that moment as much as I should have."

Edan Lepucki's *California* also went to auction, and she says she felt happy about that, but mostly because of the relationship she'd developed with her agent. Remember that Edan's agent, Erin Hosier, had signed on to represent her even after telling her she couldn't sell her first manuscript. She had to wait until Edan's next manuscript—*California*—was ready to go to make a sale. "It sold at auction in just a week or two," says Edan. "She'd been my agent for three years at that point, and had stuck with me and believed in me that whole time. And I hadn't made her a dime, so it was nice to say, 'Hey look, I sold a book!'"

Perhaps the only thing better than an auction sale is a pre-empt sale, which means a publisher offers a large amount to make sure they don't lose the book at auction. Cynthia Bond's *Ruby* was bought in a pre-empt, which she takes some credit for, but she also credits the reputation of her agent. "Nicole is the kind of agent that will open a lot of doors. She put the word out, and the very next morning Hogarth wanted to buy it in a pre-empt. When she told me the offer,

I just started crying. You put so much work into all this, and pray that it will happen, but you never know for sure. So when it happened, I was just overcome."

To sell *No Baggage*, Clara Bensen and her agent Stacy Testa developed a book proposal. Clara did significant research on comparable titles and wrote sample chapters, and when they were both happy with it, Stacy shopped it around.

It took less than a month to sell the book, and the process was handled through matter-of-fact emails, according to Clara. She remembers this time as marked more by contracts and signatures than parties and champagne toasts. Just a few days later, with a contract in hand and not much of the book even written, she learned that the film option for the book sold as well.

For Clara that was both an exciting blessing and a challenge. She was in the quite unusual situation of working with a screenwriter based on a book she hadn't yet written. "So I would finish these terrible draft chapters and send them to him, and he would take bits and pieces from them."

Did the idea of having a movie made about a book she was still writing influence her process? Clara doesn't think so. "The screenplay is an adaptation, and I refused to read anything that he was writing while I was writing. I've been really good at compartmentalizing that."

But looking back now, Clara wishes she had taken a little more time to celebrate these successes. She says with all the moments of doubt and anxiety that can drag a writer down, it's important to celebrate the successes too.

Courtney Maum doesn't remember much celebrating either. Facing a deadline from her agent, she forged ahead rewriting her ten-year-old manuscript. But she had an even more pressing deadline ahead of her: the birth of her first child. She didn't know exactly how her life would change when she had her baby, but she knew it would. After ten years of keeping the manuscript in a box, and years when she was certain this story would never be published, she saw the months before giving birth as a last chance to actually get the book out in the world.

She says she has never worked as hard on a project than in those months—and she finished the manuscript just a few weeks before the baby was due. Her agent told her a couple of publishing houses seemed interested, so she was fairly certain the book would sell at some point, but she didn't expect it when the call actually came. "I was a month away from giving birth, and it was summer and really hot, and I'd been down in the river swimming. So I came back to the house, and my agent called, and I was actually—well, I was naked on my couch when I found out." Courtney remembers that moment as one of relief more than of celebration.

Alan Heathcock strategized with his agent, Sarah Burnes, to try to land *Volt* with the right publisher. He was ready to pitch the collection at around the same time he'd been accepted to the prestigious Bread Loaf writers' conference. His good friend Benjamin Percy had nominated him for that, and "he, being Ben Percy, said he would do me bodily harm if I didn't go."

When Sarah and Alan talked about *Volt*, the first publisher that came to mind was Graywolf Press. As luck would have it, Graywolf's publisher, Fiona McCrae, was attending Bread Loaf that year. Alan cautions that while his publishing story now seems somewhat charmed, "I'd received more than two hundred rejections, and I had banged my head for a long, long time."

Alan's agent gave him an assignment for the Bread Loaf conference: try to connect with Fiona McCrae. On the first night, before he even knew what she looked like, Alan was part of the scholar reading and read a short section from his story "Smoke." Afterward Fiona walked up to him and said, "I really loved your reading. Do you have other stories?" A few weeks later, Alan had a book deal with Graywolf.

He recognizes that was a special moment, not likely to be experienced by many other writers. But he does believe he'd done the work to put himself in a position where something like that could happen.

That moment, he muses, is a reminder that writers need to put themselves out there. You just never know where a meaningful connection might be made.

So in the traditional publishing world, the point when a manuscript sells can range from overwhelming to routine. If there's a pattern, it's that many of our authors regret not taking the time to celebrate this moment a bit more. It's a great achievement for any writer, but it can get wrapped up into other anxieties, deadlines, pressures, and an overwhelming sense of relief. "Take the time to celebrate that moment," says Cynthia Bond. "It's a big deal no matter how it happens."

All the traditionally published authors knew a sale might be on the horizon. For those who go the self-publishing route, however, the "point of sale" is something simultaneously more and less involved: it's the moment a single reader rewards the author's leap into a great unknown with a purchase. Yes, the self-published author avoids some of the moments of rejection, but that's only because all the gatekeeping hurdles are rolled into one place, the marketplace.

Monona Wali tried to sell her work the traditional way, but that route did not work out for her. When she self-published her book, she sold copies to friends, family, and colleagues. But she remembers the most significant moment as being when she noticed a sale outside of her circle of influence. Someone purchased the book through Amazon, and the sale came from Nebraska, a state where she knew no one. Though Monona was a successful teacher and filmmaker, she hadn't yet been comfortable calling herself a novelist. Whether that person in Nebraska ever read the book, or loved or hated it, that purchase signified a big moment for Monona. She finally felt like she could call herself a novelist and believe what she was saying.

The Steps in Between

Once your book is sold to a publisher or you decide to self-publish, or even when you have a final manuscript ready to go, there are still numerous steps before publication—quiet steps that most authors don't always know to expect. "It's a weird dark period in publishing," says Brian Benson. "I mean you sell your book, you have an editor, you've worked on it, and then it's fifteen months until it comes out. But there are a lot of things to do, and sometimes you don't even know you should be doing them: set up a website and a Twitter account, start writing blog posts, connect on social media, and get used to talking about yourself a lot. Which is really hard."

It isn't all about platform building and promotion either. There are decisions that need to be made. For Brian, it meant a title change. From the moment he wrote page one on that first day in the coffee shop, his book was going to be titled "Outside the Mile." Then he got an email from his editor. "Her boss said she was really excited about the book but the title sounded too much like Lance Armstrong's second book, which was about performance and training your body."

Brian had thought they were done with changes, and this was a big one. He loved his title, and giving it up was preceded by a few days of "mouth breathing and stomping around." But he finally turned his attention back to a title change. He'd been reading a lot of David Foster Wallace at the time, and the first title he submitted got quickly rejected: "A Place Very Close to Wherever the Hell We Were Going." But the words from that title stuck in his mind as he reread some of the opening chapters, and he began to notice that the phrase 'going somewhere' appeared again and again in the manuscript. "Enough that I removed a bunch of them after we retitled it."

As you'll recall, besides the usual pressure of getting a book ready to publish, three of the authors profiled for this book were pushed by the deadline of pregnancy. For Rebecca Makkai, that deadline loomed as she addressed her ending. "I was really glad they pushed me, because I'm so much happier with the ending I landed on. My original ending was much too bleak. It was funny, the big pressure to get them the revised ending before my baby came. So I finished the copyedits one night and checked into the hospital the next day for my C-section."

Whether personal or arbitrary, deadlines can be useful, but sometimes they can also be frightening. In Delilah Dawson's case, her manuscript had sold, but she hadn't heard anything from the publisher in months, not even the editing notes that were promised her. She reached out to her agent, Kate, wondering if the house had forgotten about her. It hadn't, but her acquiring editor had left the publishing house. This is not that uncommon an event.

"They call it being orphaned," says Delilah. "It's terrifying for a writer because it's quite possible that your book will never see the light of day. They have to pay you your advance, but they don't have to publish your book. So it's a very scary moment."

Luckily for Delilah, another editor at the same house took on her book. Having a new editor was a relief, but Delilah still didn't hear back for a time, and she didn't know if the new editor would share the same vision as the one who acquired her book. So she anxiously waited for the new editorial letter. It turned out that she really liked working with her new editor. Despite some fairly intense turnaround expectations once the editorial letter finally came, Delilah was relieved to still have a home for her first book, and she quickly got to work.

Early in the process, Delilah realized that you have to be flexible to make it all work. At each stage—when you sign with an agent, when you get a book contract—you enter into a stable of horses; at least that's how Delilah looks at it. "You think when you get a book deal that you are the big cheese, that you're going to have a tour bus and billboards at Madison Square Garden, but you're just another one of the six hundred books being published that year. And even if they like you, unless you're like the one lucky horse that they're backing in this year's race, you're definitely going to be doing most of it on your own out of the starting gate."

Other aspects of that "weird dark period," as Brian Benson called it, include things like fact-checking, obtaining permissions, receiving proofs or galleys for proofreading, checking the formatting, requests for author bios and photos, and then of course seeing the cover. "I was tethered to my computer and phone for like a year while we got the book ready," says Courtney Maum.

She remembers one call in particular that led to a lot of anxiety. When she signed her book contract, she had told her agent that the one thing she would have liked to add to it was that the publisher couldn't put the Eiffel Tower on the cover: "You know, some woman in high heels in front of the Eiffel Tower—I'm not having that happen."

But her final cover does have an Eiffel Tower. A somewhat sheepish Rebecca Gradinger called Courtney to explain that she'd be receiving an email with the cover image, and the image did have an Eiffel Tower on it. "I started to swear," says Courtney. "But she said, 'Just look at it; it really makes sense.'"

Courtney went to her computer, dreading what she'd see. But she opened it and loved it immediately. It was obvious to her that the designer had read the book, and using the Eiffel Tower as a postage stamp was an inventive way to suggest Paris without being too obvious. She had only one request. Her name was in a difficult-to-read cursive script. "I thought, 'Well, this is my debut novel; my name should probably be more legible.'"

For a self-published author, all of those decisions come much faster because the author has total control. But with that total control comes a lot more work. Every step of the process needs a careful eye, and authors like Monona Wali also have to decide what they're willing to spend money on and what they want to do themselves.

As discussed earlier, Monona had already hired professional editorial help. She'd worked through those revisions and considered the manuscript ready to go, but that still left things like finding the right publishing platform, developing typesetting, and designing a cover.

Monona started by looking at the large self-publishing avenues, but while researching them she learned that they wouldn't necessarily walk her through every step of the process. For the bulk of the work, Monona turned to a friend of a friend who had just started a book design company named Blue Jay Ink out of Ojai, California. Blue Jay Ink typeset Monona's book, got it ready to distribute, and pulled the book together.

For the book cover, Monona turned to someone closer to home. One daughter designed her cover, and another daughter took the author photo. Monona was delighted to include her daughters in a project that was so important to her. In the end, she couldn't be happier with the whole package. "When you're doing everything yourself, you get complete control over it. I wanted a nice-looking product, but also one that meant something to me." Turning to a small local company to lay out her book, while also involving people close to her, was the perfect way to bring her book to life.

Publicity and Promotion

Promotion, publicity, and platforms are all things that debut authors are supposed to be thinking about, especially in this quiet period. And many don't even know where to begin.

Clara Bensen certainly didn't. When her *Salon* article went viral, she didn't have social media accounts beyond Facebook. After she signed with her agent, Stacy Testa, at Writers House, Stacy connected Clara with a staffer at the agency who helps coach new authors. She advised Clara on what she needed to do in building her website and developing her social media presence. Clara says the advice was invaluable, but the activities still don't come naturally to her. "I had to create a public persona for myself and actively participate in it all the time. And that can be really challenging for an introvert or a private person."

Many other authors needed to ramp up their social media presence as they were getting ready for their book release. One exception was Delilah Dawson. She had already built a large and active following, particularly on Twitter. She had started on Twitter early in her writing career, before she'd landed an agent or published anything, and began to learn and connect through the conversations there.

She continues to develop that strong following. But she cautions against trying to develop a following for the purpose of directly selling your work. Her Twitter presence keeps growing because it is authentic to who she is, and she continues to engage in meaningful conversations and interactions in that space without resorting to hard sales for her books.

"If someone comes to me and asks, 'How do I sell books on Twitter?,' I usually say, 'You can't.' It's not how it works. People don't want to see seventeen posts a day with your Amazon book link. Your goal has to be about developing genuine interactions with other human beings instead of 'me me me, look at my stuff, me me me, come buy my stuff.'"

Beyond social media, many authors worked with the marketing and publicity teams from their publishing house. Cynthia Bond had a lot of help from the promotions team as she prepared for *Ruby* to come out. They set up a number of interviews and placed a full-page ad in the *New York Times* book review section. She knows she was lucky on that level. "Nicole told me that they did things that aren't normally done."

But even without massive efforts like that, the marketing teams helped many of the authors. Brian Benson recalls that Plume helped set up his tour, arranged interviews, and helped him market his book through blog posts. Still, a significant portion of the legwork was his own, and he does have a few regrets or lessons learned. "If I had to do it again, I think I would be more shameless around the launch time. I didn't really realize just how crucial it is — that first month when your book comes out. That's when people are going to care about it in the biggest way, so it needs to be a big ramp-up before then. And I don't think I did enough of that work in advance to get there."

Rebecca Makkai also has some regrets about her involvement in getting the word out. At the time, she says, she didn't have a clue what she was doing. Now that she's observed other writer friends as well as her own subsequent books, she has a better handle on how to approach upcoming publication. She now plots out several topical essays that relate to the book to pitch to online venues. She also tries to do as many interviews as possible. She sets up Facebook events in advance of each book reading and connects with someone local to be in conversation with her as part of the reading, in order to draw more people.

Monona Wali had to do publicity all on her own, and she really focused on it being hyper-local. She let all her friends and family know about the launch and set up a reading at a local bookstore. Then she used every channel she could think of—email, Facebook, flyers—to invite people to the launch. "So my focus was really local," she says. "But that initial launch was very well attended."

Finally, Alan Heathcock learned a significant lesson while promoting his book. He describes himself as having two distinct sides, artist Al and businessman Al, and before the book came out, he says, artist Al was filled with dread. "Not because I thought the book would not be received well in terms of craft; it was more that I was realizing that the content of the book was in conflict with my public persona. People who know me think of me as happy-go-lucky and a little goofy." Friends would say to him, "I can't wait to read your book—I bet it will be hilarious."

Alan's anxiety deepened as he started promoting it. During interviews he was very hesitant to talk about his book's content because he didn't want to scare away potential readers. He'd talk about it in vague terms, with responses like "Well, it's about tough people in tough times."

But after his launch party, when his book had been out for only a few days, people started approaching him to talk about the book. In his first few readings in Boise, Idaho, and Portland, Oregon, he met people who had driven more than a hundred miles just to hear him read. They told him about people close to them who had experienced the hardship, grief, and injustice that Alan wove into his stories.

"After I started making all these connections, I had this shift in my thinking. My job in talking about this book was exactly the opposite of where I started. I can't nip at the edges and speak in vague generalities. My job is to say exactly what the book is, in all of its harshness and darkness, because there are people in the world who are looking for that exact book. It cut across all kinds of lives and demographics. People wanted to read about and talk about the things that we don't often talk about."

So he changed his outreach, the way he spoke in his interviews, and how he described the book. As the next chapter will show, those changes led to some meaningful connections for Alan.

As our authors discovered, the period preceding the book's publication is a fluid time to prepare, promote, celebrate — and start to consider what kind of project comes next.

What to Expect When Publishing

The exact steps in the process leading up to publication vary depending on whether you're publishing traditionally (and within that world, what type of publisher you're working with) or doing it yourself, but here are some of the most common steps in publishing your first book.

Developmental Edits

In most cases, the first step will be for the submitted manuscript to go through a developmental edit. This typically involves an editor reading the manuscript and sending the author a developmental edit letter, with suggestions for additions, revisions, cuts, and changes. Many self-publishing outfits are now offering this as a paid service as well.

Permissions and Fact-Checking

Depending on the nature of the manuscript, you may need to comply with legal requirements such as obtaining permissions or fact-checking early in the process

Copyedits and Typesetting

Once the manuscript gets through the developmental process, it will most typically enter the copyedit phase. This usually involves a careful edit for details such as grammar and punctuation, laying out and typesetting of the pages, proofreading of the typeset pages, and creation of any indexes or appendices.

Cover Design

At some point, usually during the copyediting phase, you will see a cover design concept. If you self-publish, you'll have total say in how this looks and can hire your own designer. If you publish traditionally, the amount of say you have will vary tremendously depending on the project, but generally you won't have a lot of influence on this process.

Acknowledgments, Bio, and Head Shots

You will be asked to provide acknowledgments, and the marketing department will solicit your most recent bio and some head shots.

Advance Reader Copies and Publicity

Once the work is typeset, the publisher will typically make advance reader copies available. The author may use these to try to obtain blurbs, to pitch to reviewers and bloggers for reviews and articles, or to connect with potential booksellers. It's also during this period that an author will plan the book launch, as well as build up the digital presence of their new book.

10. The Book in the World

At last comes the long fought-for and awaited day—larva into butterfly, idea into book. The hours of effort, the many obstacles, the thoughts of abandonment, the compromises, and the determination all become something tangible. But the work doesn't stop there, and something else interesting happens: this thing that had been a relatively private obsession becomes a public commodity.

Every aspiring writer dreams about praise and public rewards—someone buying and reading their book, maybe even enough someones to make it a best seller. But there's much more to the public nature of a book than the sales, and for some of our authors, those other public aspects—the critics, the internet reviews, the launch parties, the increased attention, the personal connections with readers—took them by surprise.

Moreover, a new sensation arrived with their new public face. Many of our authors talked about the feeling that the work was no longer solely theirs. Now nothing about their book could change: it sat fixed in a moment as something the writer felt strangely separated from. It belonged to the readers now, and our authors had to find their path forward to the next project.

The Book Launch

For some of our authors, getting that first book out into the world was an exciting, happy time; for others it brought stress and self-doubt along with the upbeat moments.

Each writer planned his or her own launch party. For some a book tour followed the launch, while others focused more on publicity and interviews. But one recommendation that seemed consistent across the group was to make sure you plan a launch that fits you.

For Delilah Dawson, her book launch was a big deal. It was a moment of validation. "I have no MFA, no certification. I did not go to New York to schmooze at parties, and I did all this in my pajamas."

So when she planned it, she decided to go big. She invited family and longtime friends. She hired a bakery to make a "ginormous" cake. She went in costume. She made jewelry that could be won in a raffle. She created special labels for the bottles of wine to reflect the world of the book. It took a lot of time and energy, but she doesn't regret it.

"I feel like you should do whatever makes you happy when you launch that first time. I never had that sparkling moment at prom or homecoming. So this was my moment where I planned every aspect of that party, and there were people there I hadn't seen in years."

The big party felt to Delilah like her arrival as an author. Though she hasn't held another one like that for subsequent books, it's an important milestone that she looks back on fondly. It also helps her as she works on subsequent projects. "You don't need to do this, you don't need to have a massive party. It just needs to fit you and your book. But I am so glad I did it because I look at those pictures sometimes, and I can see the incandescent joy on my face, and it reminds me, if I've forgotten, just how magical this writing life can be."

Brian Benson also tried to fit his book launch to his story. He biked his book tour. That decision turned out to be a good one, because it fed publicity. Numerous interviews and media stories followed. Not only did biking fit the book, but it was a low-budget way to do a ten-reading tour. And that's helpful these days, when most authors cover their own costs or have to skip the book tour altogether.

Brian says the tour also helped him deal with the emotional pressures of his book launch, which he grew anxious about as the day approached. "It was the idea of people reading it, and that it might get terrible reviews, or people hating it and hating me forever. If I wasn't out on the road biking, I would've been in my room refreshing my Amazon and Goodreads pages, basing my entire sense of self-worth on how the numbers fared. So being out there really helped me deal with all that anxiety."

Brian's advice to aspiring writers is similar to Delilah's when it comes to the book launch. "Make it personal." But he also advises making the process an experience. The more you can avoid sitting at home alone watching how the book fares on the internet, he says, the better off you'll be.

Many of the authors profiled for this book organized a party and reading. Clara Bensen, Monona Wali, Courtney Maum, Eric Smith, and Cynthia Bond all recalled an amazing night. For each of them, it was a culmination of years of work—a big high. However, many did not expect how fleeting that feeling might be. "When you put a book out, it's this wonderful flash," says Monona. "It was just such a high, and I was so happy I'd decided to self-publish when it came out. But you know that ends. Pretty quickly too, and then you have to just go back to facing the blank page and trying to keep learning from where you've been."

Clara Bensen launched *No Baggage* at independent bookstore Book People in Austin, Texas. She reports that it was a magical night, filled with friends, family, and a real sense of accomplishment. But she also remembers a moment from that night when she first saw her book on the shelf. "I definitely had the sensation that it was no longer mine anymore, to the point that it was almost like there was some other Clara Bensen who wrote the book that's on the shelf."

The high that came from that evening faded quickly, too. In the next days and weeks she did what Brian Benson recommends against and started to watch her sales. At the time of our interview, Clara's book had been out about two months. Sales had been good, but not runaway. "The other thing that surprised me is that if giving birth is part of the metaphor, I've also experienced postpartum depression now. The publicity wave has subsided, and this thing that I spent two and a half years of my life writing is now done. And the world keeps spinning, and what now? So there's a slump afterward that I wasn't expecting."

Here's a writer who had a fairly charmed path to publication. A viral article, agents seeking her out, and a publishing and movie deal before she'd written a word of the book. Even in her positive circumstances, the quiet that follows publication can be a challenge. Clara wishes she'd been more prepared for the business aspects of the book's release. "I now have a much greater awareness of how much writing is a business. As a writer, you have to be able to shift between artist and businesswoman. You also have to realize that publishing is a gamble. Even if you get an agent, even if you get a publisher, even if your book is on a shelf, it's still an uphill climb."

Cynthia Bond found herself in that uphill climb when *Ruby* came out, and she likewise remembers not being prepared for it. As the setbacks chapter revealed, many of her national newspaper reviews fell through when it came out, and thus her sales were quite low relative to the advance she'd received. Cynthia was excited for the launch, but she wasn't prepared for the switch she'd have to make. "When it came out, I was very surprised how much you left the creative process and entered this business and marketing process."

She says Amazon and Goodreads are like "radioactive toxic waste" for a debut author: if you dig deep enough, you can find every kind of insult and criticism. She was prepared for that. She just wasn't prepared for the quiet that followed *Ruby*'s publication. "Being ignored was one of the most painful things I'd ever lived through. It was my life's work, and it wasn't being ripped apart, it was being ignored."

Maybe the only thing worse than being ignored as you prepare to publish is being caught up in a turf war between corporations. Edan Lepucki spent years writing her debut book after giving up on a first novel that had also taken years to write. As the launch date for *California* approached, the world's largest marketplace for books suddenly made it extremely difficult to buy her book. The 2014 dispute over ebook pricing emerged between Amazon and Edan Lepucki's publisher Hachette (the parent company of Little, Brown), and all the Hachette authors were caught up in something completely beyond their control.

The two companies could not resolve their differences, so Amazon began subjecting Hachette books to artificial purchase delays, sometimes up to five weeks for books that had previously been available for next-day delivery. In other cases Hachette books wouldn't even show up in Amazon searches. At the time Amazon accounted for 41 percent of all new book sales. With initial sales being crucial for debut authors, lack of access on Amazon could potentially kill a book.

As her publication date drew closer and the standoff intensified, Edan grew increasingly anxious about her debut's prospects. It didn't help matters that her husband works for Goodreads, an Amazon company. "It was all so stressful," says Edan. "This is the thing I've wanted my whole life more than anything. And I was like, this is getting fucked by *this*? You're already anxious about your book, but this, it's just so out of your hands. It was just horrible."

While she fretted about what it all meant for her book, she did continue to plan her own launch readings in New York, San Francisco, and Los Angeles. She also worked on writing and placing essays in publications like *The Millions*, among other publicity efforts. But as she worked on those readings, essays, and interviews, and worried about the dispute, she had little idea that everything was about to change even more dramatically.

The Outside Help

When all seemed lost for Edan, the Amazon and Hachette dispute took quite a turn for her. Just as *California* was about to launch, Edan got a call from her publicist. "She sounded like she was drunk, she was just so giddy."

It just so happened that Stephen Colbert's books were also published by Hachette, and he was featuring the dispute on his Comedy Central show *The Colbert Report*. Since debut novelists were going to be hurt the most by this dispute, Colbert invited Sherman Alexie onto his show to feature a debut novel by a Hachette author. Together, they would urge Colbert's audience to buy it through independent bookseller Powell's.

Sherman Alexie called Edan and told her that he wanted to feature her book because he liked the story and thought it would appeal to the most people. "I was really excited because it was national exposure, but I also didn't really think it was going to make that much of a difference. I thought we might sell forty extra copies, my husband said four hundred. But then it kind of went crazy after that."

The show aired. Edan admits that in the quietest corner of her heart, she had wanted to be on a best-seller list someday. She also says she felt a little guilty to be finding success in a situation that was still difficult for so many other writers. But most of her writer friends were very supportive rather than envious. Her book became a rallying emblem of the struggles of debut novelists caught in an impossible situation.

She had been wrong about the impact of her book's appearance on *The Colbert Report*. That same week Edan found herself at Powell's Books signing ten thousand copies of *California*. Hachette printed sixty thousand hardcover copies of the book instead of the originally planned print run of twelve thousand. A *New York Times* profile was written about her. She appeared on Colbert's show later that month to pick another debut novel—she selected Stephan Eirik Clark's *Sweetness #9*. And *California* landed at number 3 on the *New York Times* best-seller list.

As Edan found herself and her book swept up in a cultural moment, she felt honored and amazed. But some quiet part of her also felt a little wary. The *New York Times* profile about her led with the line "Nobody expected much from Edan Lepucki's debut novel," and while Edan says she's eternally grateful for the coverage and genuinely liked the reporter who wrote that article, she was uncomfortable being thought of as some hapless writer who just got lucky. "My book sold at auction. Little, Brown put a lot behind it. So it's not like I just stumbled into this," she says. "Still, no doubt once Colbert put his muscle behind it, it was clear that I was on a different plane."

In that same vein, when all seemed lost, Cynthia Bond received a call that dramatically changed *Ruby*'s prospects. Cynthia calls her period of losing reviews and sinking sales a "personal hell." In the midst of that time, her phone rang. Cynthia remembers picking up the phone with defeat in her voice. "In this nadir of my professional life, with my voice carrying a lot of misery and pain, I get this call out of the blue, and it was Oprah Winfrey on the line. Not an assistant, but Oprah. She called to say that she loved my book and that she wanted to make it her book club pick."

There was one stipulation: Cynthia couldn't tell anyone. They would announce it through the magazine and on Oprah's show. So while her sales continued to drag, as friends and acquaintances continued to ask Cynthia how her book was selling, she had to keep her lips sealed. Except for her mother, she says: "I did have to just tell her."

A week later Cynthia was flown out for a magazine photo shoot, and she met Oprah Winfrey too. *Ruby* was coming out in paperback, so they planned to announce the book club pick on the same day it released. "Then the day it came out, it was just this insane, crazy press. A few weeks later *Ruby* was on the *New York Times* best-seller list. Then she had me on her show and her film studio optioned *Ruby*, and now I'm writing the screenplay for that."

Cynthia looks back on the Oprah pick, and all the attention and sales that followed, as a kind of wakeup call. She's absolutely grateful for all the new readers she's been able to connect with, but she realizes now that she paid too much attention to those external marketplace forces. She was anxious about the future of her other manuscripts when *Ruby* wasn't selling well, but the success after the Oprah pick didn't change her thinking about the book. Poor sales can happen to really good books, and Cynthia realizes now that she was letting that cloud her vision. "It was just as good a book when it was selling poorly as when it was a best seller. It's important to remember that."

It may not have brought the fame that Oprah or Colbert could provide, but Monona Wali had lightning strike for *My Blue Skin Lover* too. In 2015 her book was awarded the Independent Publisher Book Award's Gold Medal for Multicultural Fiction. Since most of the major awards exclude self-published works from consideration, this award series is one of the most significant ones that self-published authors can receive. While it won't have the same result as an Oprah Book Club pick, it can have a significant effect.

It was also a validating moment for Monona. "It was just a great, wonderful surprise to get that award for the book," she says. "And it was huge because it was this completely independent award — much like the validation that comes when a publisher says yes. It's the same effect. Somebody else is saying your book is worthy. It was not my friends, not my network, it was somebody else saying this book is really great."

Monona saw the immediate effect, both in terms of sales and in the number of online reviews she began receiving. It was clear that more people were connecting with her book.

But not every response to a book can be an Oprah pick or win a big award. The most frequent response most writers see is reviews by critics or readers. Dealing with them can turn out to be an important skill for a debut author.

Rebecca Makkai received a number of starred reviews for *The Borrower* before it came out. But she says she didn't really know what that meant or how big of a deal it was to get several of those. So those successes more or less washed over her, and instead she found herself focused on a single review.

It was a largely negative review in the industry trade magazine *Publishers Weekly* — negative enough that it prompted her agent, Nicole Aragi, to call Rebecca before she read it. Even though Nicole tried to talk Rebecca through it, she remembers being fairly inconsolable. "I felt like that one review meant my book was dead in the water, no one was going to read it. I have thicker skin now, but I also have much more perspective now on how much good or damage one review can do to you, or for you. At the time I wish I would've known all that, because it just felt like it was everything: I'd been found out as a fraud and my career was over."

Brian Benson also had to come to terms with a review. The hardest part was that it seemed like the reviewer hadn't even read his book. "One of the first reviews that came out was pretty scathing. There were a lot of factual inaccuracies in the review, and that was especially hard. You put so much time and heart into writing something, and you don't get to control who reviews it or how your book is reviewed. Even if they say they hated things that didn't appear in your book, you don't have any control over it, and still that can become a very big shaping narrative for how your book is received."

In the future Brian plans to avoid reading his reviews. He says if they're good, they go to your head; if they're bad, you can't do anything about it. Clara Bensen seconds that approach. She decided at the very beginning that she wouldn't read a single review. Not from book critics and not from readers, neither in print nor online. "Even if it was titled 'Clara Bensen Is the Most Awesome Writer in the World,' I wouldn't read it. That's the biggest way I created distance between myself and the finished product. I mean, I can't go back and edit it. It's out there. It's done. It's time to move on."

Connecting with Readers

When a book comes out, authors need to adjust to the public reaction, and either ignore it or find a way to thicken their skin. But there is another side to this, the sometimes surprising and unpredictable ways that readers react personally to the authors' books. And these moments can brighten even the worst days.

Our authors noted two things that surprised them about interacting with their readers. One, just *how* gratifying and sustaining it can be, and two, that it can take up a lot of time. Many of the authors pointed out that finding a balance is an important skill to develop because sometimes the reader outreach gets overwhelming. In the weeks and months after their debut books came out, most of our authors set up specific times to respond to readers. It helped them keep that part of their writing life from taking over.

But that doesn't mean they didn't appreciate it. In fact, Brian Benson told me how important it was to hear from readers after *Going Somewhere* came out. "My motivation for writing anything is to connect emotionally with readers. So to hear from someone who read it, liked it, and took the time to write me about it has been the best part of the process. I don't know if readers understand how meaningful that is to an author. Writing is a lonely thing. Publishing is a lonely thing. To be able to bring it out of that sphere is just so meaningful."

For Delilah Dawson, some of the most surprising aspects of reader connections were the gifts she started to receive. In the week her book came out, she received a package. It didn't have a return address and she didn't recognize it. "I was like 'Someone has just mailed me a bomb.' But I opened it anyway, and someone had knitted a Blud Bunny."

The Blud Bunnies are an important part of the world in *Wicked as They Come*—so much so that for her launch party, Delilah had a life-size Blud Bunny created. "She must have read it the day it came out and made this for me. That's how much she loved it. I don't even know how she did it, but I was a very lonely kid, and having people want to connect with me is still very new and pretty awesome."

A painting of a blue bear plays a crucial part throughout Courtney Maum's novel. More than a year after her book had come out, she received a painting of a blue bear from a reader who loved it. "That was super cool. You've moved on, and sometimes you feel like no one's reading the book anymore, so when you get something like that, it's just so nice to be reminded that it is still out there and people are still connecting with it."

For Monona Wali, it was hearing from one particular reader that meant the most. "I wrote a weird little book about a woman who takes the god Shiva as her lover, and for whatever reason I was compelled to tell that story. But I did sometimes wonder whether it would resonate with others." After it came out, Monona's father gave the book to a friend of his. Monona has great respect for this man and didn't know that her father had shared the book with him. One day she saw that she had three messages from him on her phone and wondered if there was an emergency. But he'd just been eagerly trying to reach her. "He absolutely loved the book. When I finally did reach him, he said, 'I just want to start it all over again and read it again and again.'"

She had never imagined this ninety-year-old classical piano teacher as part of the audience for her book. For Monona, that was what stuck with her—and other unlikely readers emerged. "I have several experiences like that with people who I never imagined liking the book, liking it."

The number of people who purchased *California* in response to the Stephen Colbert and Sherman Alexie interview was large. It also meant that a lot of people reviewed Edan Lepucki's book, and some weren't so kind. One day Edan's husband caught her reading all of her one-star reviews on Amazon and Goodreads, and he asked her why she was doing that to herself.

She told him she wanted to hear criticism so she could improve her next work. She understands that you can't try to write a book that everyone will like, and she loves many books that other people— even people she respects—hate. But as an intellectual exercise, she thought it might be useful to try to identify any trends that might be helpful as she wrote her next books.

It wasn't helpful. Most of the reviews weren't filled with constructive ways to think about her work; many reviewers were just upset that her book had rocketed to the best-seller list based on a television show. Worse, several reviews were particularly mean-spirited personal attacks on her, and they took their toll on Edan. "I had to learn not to look at those reviews. If my book's not for them, that's fine, but I don't need to read why I'm an awful person for writing it."

It was in the days after reading those reviews that Edan most clearly remembers hearing positively from a reader. She was at a party hosted by a friend when someone walked up to her and asked, "Are you Edan Lepucki?" and then proceeded to tell Edan how much she loved her book. Edan says it's always a little awkward to be lavished with praise, especially at a party, but that person helped her in ways she'll never fully know. "When you hear from somebody like that, that loved your work, it's amazing. It's especially great when they connect with it the way that you wanted people to connect with it, and she was one of those readers."

Beyond praise, gifts, and validation, some of the authors connected with readers on an even more personal level. In those cases their book opened up conversations that some readers had long closed down. Alan Heathcock's first reading after his launch was at Powell's in Portland, and a woman came up to him as he was signing. She had driven an hour and half to hear him read. She said her son had been killed in a car crash, and she'd heard that Alan's book had characters dealing with immense grief. His book gave her permission to deal with some of her own grief, she said, and she drove all that way because she wanted him to know that.

"I don't know why I didn't anticipate it. And maybe it's because as Americans we don't talk that openly about the muck in our lives, but what I found was that everywhere I went, there was a woman or a man just like that. It's a very powerful and intimate connection that you gain with people. On one hand, it means I became the prince of darkness everywhere I went, but at the same time, everywhere I went I've felt more connected to people. There are people struggling with this everywhere."

His book opened up a vein of communication that didn't exist before for these readers. And other of our authors reported a similar phenomenon. For Zetta Elliott, *Bird* allowed her to talk more openly about her family and addiction. "The first time I presented at the Brooklyn Public Library, a kid asked me what inspired me, and I hadn't planned it, but I just started opening up about my brother. Afterward adults and children would come up to me and say, 'Thank you—that happened in my family too.' It opened my eyes. When you let go of silence and shame, you open up opportunities to build community."

For Clara Bensen, it was readers reaching out about their own struggles with mental health. Like Zetta and Alan, she says that talking about things we don't often talk about has opened up a space for people to share back their own experiences. Clara regularly receives letters that say things like "I don't feel I can talk about this openly, but because you did, that really helps me try."

It echoes through most of our authors' experiences. Cynthia Bond reports that after the Oprah pick, she received dozens of letters from survivors of sexual abuse. Many of the letters said things like "I don't usually reveal this, but I am Ruby. This is part of my story too."

Courtney Maum has received a number of messages and letters from readers who saw their own relationships in new lights. In particular, she heard from partners who had experienced an infidelity—both as the cheater and as the ones cheated on. They told her how much her story had meant as they tried to repair their relationships.

Reading those letters was especially powerful for Courtney because she'd read reviews from readers who didn't like the book simply because an infidelity occurred in it. She visited a few book groups where the participants accused Courtney of having defended infidelity simply by writing about it. So it meant a lot to her to hear from readers who felt that her book helped them.

Finally, there's Rebecca Makkai. She started receiving a number of emails and letters from gay men in their twenties who really identified with her character Ian. She says she'd receive two kinds of letters. The first would tell her that like ten-year-old Ian, they grew up frequently visiting the library and were gay, but their parents were great and accepted them. They told Rebecca that they gave *The Borrower* to their parents to thank them for not being like the parents in the book. This touched Rebecca quite a bit.

But the second kind of letter resonated particularly deeply with Rebecca. The letters would say, "I grew up just like Ian. My parents put me in an anti-gay camp, and this book was so cathartic." For Rebecca, who was never quite sure what kind of life the future held for her character Ian, the next parts of the letter were "very trippy. Then they'd say, 'I'm really doing good now.' Those letters were almost like getting a letter from Ian himself, who had become real to me and who I had come to really care about. To get a letter that felt like him writing me to say, 'Hey, it's me, I've moved forward, and I'm doing fine now' was really pretty incredible."

The Next Project

The sophomore effort can sometimes be more demanding than the first. There are new external pressures and more people counting on the second book, including a group of readers who supported the first. The second work also may bring inner doubts that can block the process. These challenges are only heightened if the first book found any commercial or critical success.

So how do you prepare for the second-book jitters? Here's some advice from our authors.

Accept the Challenge

Even if you have a first book out or coming out in the world, don't assume the next project will be easier. Yes, you'll have developed a process through that first work, but you'll have to learn and explore new things for the second. As Courtney Maum put it, the only thing she learned writing her first book was how to write her first book. She says it's like starting over completely with the second book. These issues are manageable; it's just helpful to know that going in. Decide you're up for the challenge.

Expect to Slump

Several of the authors spoke about experiencing an emotional low after the end of the first-book fanfare, reviews, and interviews. They then had to return to the rather lonely process of putting words to page. Authors such as Clara Bensen, Delilah Dawson, and Cynthia Bond all said that they weren't prepared for that feeling of isolation, and it hurt their process when they jumped back into the next project. They said you probably can't avoid it, but if they'd expected it, they might have been able to move forward more quickly.

Start It Early

As pointed out, there are quiet periods during the publishing process for a debut book. You may be waiting to hear back from an editor or a publicist. And though you likely deserve a little time off, many of the authors recommend writing anyway. They said your anxiety grows before the first book launches, and after it's out, the time pressures grow for a second book. Many of the writers found it helpful to start the second work before the first was released.

You Can't Go Back

Some first books come out to mixed or quiet reviews, or they sell less than expected. On the business side, that can make selling the next book harder. Other first books come out to accolades, great reviews, interview requests, and even strikes of lightning like awards or Oprah picks or being featured by Stephen Colbert.

Either side of this can cause apprehension or fear when you are approaching your next project. To a person, every author interviewed for this book pointed out that you can't go back to the first book; all you can do is write the next one and do it as best you can. The rest is out of your hands. As Edan Lepucki says, "I'm writing as if that will never happen again. I was clear with myself even while it was happening. As long as I focus on the next book rather than the one I already wrote, my head stays clear and focused."

11. Lessons Learned

So what have we learned from our lineup of debut authors? Each book is different, and each takes a different path that must be discovered and cultivated. You can't just copy a successful path to publication and expect it to be the same for you.

That said, there are many widely applicable lessons to be drawn from the experiences of these authors. For example, the authors may have found the ideas behind their books in unique ways, but they were all fully open to the hard work in chasing down those ideas. In their writing process, they remained receptive to experimenting and trying new tactics. In their support networks, they found a multitude of people ready to help them on their journey, or they regretted the solo difficulties when they didn't. In developing craft, themes, and structure for their work, many authors found ways to meticulously track or chart the book's elements and their revisions. And when it came to publishing, they persevered through countless doubts and setbacks, researched the options before them, and pushed forward despite the barriers.

Each of our authors now has a debut work behind them. The books have found varied degrees of success, but all helped propel the writers' careers forward. The books are out, finding their readers, and the authors return to them every so often with a question from an interviewer or someone at a reading. All of the debuts profiled for this book were published since 2007, most more recently than that, and many of the authors have now published a second, third, or—in Delilah Dawson's case—tenth book since their debut.

Even the authors who haven't published a second work are focusing creative energies toward their next project. The debut book is now just one part of their writing arc, an artifact they look back on with fondness and, in some cases, a little remorse. In every case, they carry pieces of that debut forward with them.

Based on their experiences the first time around, our authors have evolved their approaches. Any aspiring writer can learn from that progress if we study their processes.

In my interviews with the authors, some of my questions were universal and some were tailored to each of them individually. But I intentionally ended each interview with the same two questions: (1) What lessons do you carry from your debut book into your next projects? (2) What lessons could an aspiring writer learn from your journey to publication?

Here, then, in closing, are the authors' answers to these questions in their own words. May their diverse insights help guide you wherever your journey to publication takes you.

You Can Do It

Delilah Dawson knows how daunting it can be. She knows how many roadblocks and pitfalls there are for an aspiring author. She knows how long it takes to find a publishing path, let alone a group of devoted readers, but fundamentally she believes that anyone can put their mind to it and do it.

"You don't have to be a certain age, a certain gender, a certain color. You don't have to live in a certain place, make a certain amount of money. You don't need a fancy computer or a fancy program. You don't need a degree or certification. You don't need to go to a workshop. This is more about putting in your ten thousand hours and being tenacious. Don't give up. Slog through the hard parts. All you have to do is keep writing, and get good enough to get someone's attention."

Dream Big

One thing that Rebecca Makkai continues to be proud of is that she took chances and believed in herself, no matter how slim that chance might have been. If you just assume you won't get something, and then don't even try, you'll be absolutely right.

"When I was in college, I used to open slush mail and send out rejection slips for *Shenandoah*, so I was reading a lot of cover letters. There was one letter that stuck out to me, and in retrospect maybe she used this line with everyone, but it said, 'My professor said I should always start at the top and work my way down, and that's why I'm writing you first.' I'll admit that is cheesy and likely not something you should explicitly say, but it struck a chord with me at the time.

"When I wrote Nicole, that letter was in my mind. I told myself that I had to at least try for a top agent, and then when that didn't work, I'd move down the ladder. Don't aim low because you have low expectations, and do know that rejections at the top don't mean you aren't ready."

Get Comfortable with Discomfort

The writing life isn't easy, and many delude themselves into thinking it will be different for them. No matter how talented you are or how good your idea is, there will always be aspects that push you outside your comfort zone. That's a good thing, says Monona Wali.

"The analogy I use is falling off a ship into the ocean. You will almost always feel like you're drowning, but you have to stop focusing on that feeling and know that you will make it to shore."

Purge What Holds You Back

There are so many possible things that can get in the way for an aspiring writer; Alan Heathcock just recommends that you don't let it be yourself. He admits this is easier said than done, but he's learned that it is only to your benefit to try.

"Fear, doubt, shame, or guilt: just get rid of it. Just keep doing what you're doing and move forward."

Trust Your Vision

Zetta Elliott says you need to trust your vision as an aspiring author. Rejection may mean the work needs to change or isn't quite ready yet, but sometimes it means you just haven't found the right venue. As an author, you have to ask yourself some tough questions and figure out if you believe in your work as it stands.

"Trust your vision. Defend your work if you believe in it. As writers, we all have doubts, but it's so important to stand by yourself. If you don't stand behind your work, you will be moved from your purpose. And if you don't believe in it, you'll end up with a book that might be interesting to other people, but it won't reflect your vision for the story or for the characters."

Don't Quit

Eric Smith found himself writing two very different kinds of books. Switching between *Inked* and *The Geek's Guide to Dating* presented some problems, but he remained open to all the possibilities before him. Having worked at a publishing house, and now working as an agent himself, Eric knows how difficult the publishing industry can be to break into.

"I've learned a lot being on various sides of publishing, and I think the biggest thing I've learned about the people who succeed is that they just keep trying. Take every opportunity that presents itself. To quote *Galaxy Quest*, 'Never give up, never surrender.'"

Say Yes, and Yes Again

Edan Lepucki says that after spending so much time writing your book, make sure you also do everything you can to help it flourish when it comes out. For a lot of writers that means coming out of their shells, but they should do it nonetheless.

"Do everything you can to help your book. Say yes to every interview, everything that a publicist throws your way. Do the events, smile, write thank-you notes to booksellers, be there, be public. If you hate it, still do it, and if nothing else it will help remind you how much you like to write."

Also Learn to Say No

Delilah Dawson points out that before you have a book deal, no one asks you to do anything. But once the book is coming out, and especially after it comes out, the requests can start to pile up. In many cases they aren't glamorous or paid opportunities—in Delilah's experience, people expect a debut author to do just about anything. Write for free. Come to a book club. Contribute something to a fundraiser. Introduce a reader. Write a blurb, a review, an article, an essay.

And it's not that a debut author shouldn't do those things. They should, but when the requests start to pile up and get in the way of the next project or of promoting the current one, you have to learn to prioritize and find the will to say no. "I used to get really stressed because I said yes to everything. I'd heard that's what you're supposed to do. But that can run you ragged. I had to learn how to say no."

It's Hard to Tell a Good Story

It can take years to learn to tell a good story. Monona Wali thinks you need to first accept that what you're trying to do is hard.

"It is really, really hard to tell a good story. I think that's why a lot of modern novels rely on fragmentation, because it tends to lessen that burden. But know that what you're doing is hard, and you should expect it to be so."

Be Organized

Rebecca Makkai is happy with *The Borrower*, but she regrets that it took her ten years to write it. She now outlines every novel in meticulous detail, and while she knows that doesn't work for every writer, she thinks all writers need to come up with some kind of plan for their story. For Rebecca that's an outline, but for others it may just be an idea of where they're headed and a plan for completing the work. She believes that if you just leave it to whim and chance, it will take much, much longer to complete.

"Writing a novel is never entirely linear, but you do yourself a disservice to not think about some of these things in advance. You really create a lot more work for yourself when you don't have a plan. You can be creative and structured at the same time — it's not either-or."

Never Stop Learning

Edan Lepucki still thinks about changing parts of *California*. She knows you can't do that, but she does think it's important to account for those things and make sure you work these insights into your next work.

"I learned so much from *California* — about balancing perspectives and secrets, about pacing and flashbacks. I've learned even more since *California* came out and saw how people reacted to it, and I'm trying to bring all of those lessons and techniques into my new book."

Reject Normal

As Clara Bensen points out, you can't try to catch lightning in a bottle twice, and it is important to stay dedicated and grounded. At the same time, she strongly believes that writers need to take chances and push boundaries. She believes the viral fame of her work came from tweaking a social norm, and that can be a powerful thing to explore.

"Getting on a plane without any baggage is really not that big of a deal, but people went nuts. So I've taken that idea with me in terms of my creative process, that I can try to push boundaries just slightly and have some interesting things happen. You need to be willing to go down strange paths as part of your creative process. Don't try to have any expectations about where it might lead; just have a willingness to play with the idea of normal."

Enjoy the Ride

Brian Benson cautions against thinking exclusively about the finished product. If publication is all you're in it for, he thinks you're likely to run into trouble. He encourages everyone working on a book to try to enjoy the process as much as possible.

"That physical product, the book, is honestly only 1 percent of the experience. The rest of it is writing it, editing it, and publicizing it. If you can't figure out a way to make those different parts enjoyable, you aren't going to like most parts of publishing. Writing is so much about this arduous, seemingly endless set of tasks and processes. Enjoy as much of it as you can, and even with the parts that suck, figure out a way to develop a process that feels meaningful and isn't just about that goal at the end. I think that has to exist, or you'll burn out."

Protect Yourself and Get Involved

You're the only person who will be looking out for yourself in the end. Courtney Maum reminds each writer to protect themselves. Similar to some other recommendations, she advises authors not to jump on board with the first agent that shows interest in them. She thinks one of the best ways to protect yourself as a writer is to build meaningful connections.

"I don't mean to tell people to 'lawyer up'; I just mean be careful with your decisions. The best advice I can give is to stay involved in the reading and writing community. Despite any competition or desperation you might be feeling while hearing about everyone's next massive book contract, you need to hang in there and stay connected. Subscribe to literary magazines, keep sending your work out, and find people who you trust. Be vocal about your failings and rejections, because not enough people are, and if more people were, we would be more supportive of each other instead of hiding it all the time. If we'd all just be honest about everything, the things going well and the things not, it would be a lot better."

Make Connections

Brian Benson knows all the long, lonely hours of writing his book were important, but he doubts that *Going Somewhere* would exist today without the people he met who helped him push it forward: those who encouraged him, taught him, and connected him to various other people. It's easy to focus on the writing side of things or to push back against the idea of networking to success. But Brian points out that it doesn't need to be smarmy or shallow.

"There are a lot of kind and generous people in the writing world. Like it or not, success in writing is so much about relationships. If I hadn't joined the Atheneum and had a chance to meet Karen and Cheryl, there's no chance that I would have had a publishing deal in the way that I did. Maybe someday down the road, but not in the way it happened. While writing is really a solitary thing, success in publishing is so much about getting outside your habit hole."

Find Trusted Eyes

Cynthia Bond can't emphasize enough how important it is to find the right people in your life to help you push your work forward.

"It's just so important: get your work critiqued by kind and good people. People who will be ruthless without destroying you or your work. You don't want a soft touch. You want to make your work the very best that you can make it, to the very edge of your talents, and then push it out into the world."

Find Aerial Views

If you'll remember, when she wrote a synopsis to show an agent, Rebecca Makkai began to see big holes in her story. Writing the synopsis helped her focus out on the broad view rather than the intricate details, and she advocates that every aspiring writer find a way to see their work that way. Doing it early in the process will save a lot of headaches downstream.

"That first synopsis became my first outline for *The Borrower,* so now I do that earlier, and I'm a mad outliner. I end up with a document that is showing me the landscape of the novel, but it isn't a synopsis. I'm not saying everyone needs to outline — there are many ways to get an aerial view of your work. But finding that is so crucial. If you're in the thick of writing it, you're much too close to see the shape of it, and it will lead you places you don't want to go."

Learn the Rules and Be Willing to Break Them

As an author, you owe it to yourself to learn all the options, according to Zetta Elliott. The worst thing that you can do is to go about trying to put your work out in the world blindly.

"There are multiple paths to publication, so I think it is important to know and understand the rules of the industry, so you can follow them, bend them, or break them altogether. I'm glad I've taken the many paths I've taken. If you believe you're a storyteller and you have multiple stories to tell, be open to that. I'm glad I didn't put all my eggs in one basket. I'm glad I looked into the different paths to publication, because it has put more of my stories into the world."

Don't Fear the Weird

Try not to limit your stories, especially at first. Whether you plot them out or not, Monona Wali says, the active subconscious mind must have freedom to work. The analytical side of your brain can come in while you are revising, but to begin with, allow your story to move into unexpected areas. You can always rein it in later.

"I'm very respectful of having faith in strangeness. I'd advise against shutting down the weirdness in a story you're telling, especially while drafting. Develop it and have faith in it."

Don't Stress Trends

It's just fine to observe trends, says Delilah Dawson, but you shouldn't let them govern what projects you take on. The day Delilah's book sold, she remembers opening an article on *Writer's Digest* which basically proclaimed that "vampires are dead": because of *Twilight*, the trope was over and no one would read or publish vampire stories anymore.

"From the start, I had it drilled into me that they may tell you it won't sell, but if it's good enough, it will. So anytime I've had an idea that keeps nagging at me, I'll write it anyway. Write the book that really excites and inflames you. Put everything you have into it, and you can succeed no matter what the industry is telling you the trends are."

Take Your Time

There's tremendous pressure to publish, to find an agent, and to get your career rolling. And sometimes that pressure can cause you to make poor decisions. Take a long view when making decisions on where you submit and who to work with. That can be hard when you've dealt with rejection, but if you find yourself stuck in the wrong place or relationship, it can be even worse.

"I have so many writer friends who regretted signing with the first agent that showed any interest in them. And it really set them back. It's like marrying the first guy you kissed just because he kissed you. It just might not be the best match," says Edan Lepucki.

Prepare for Intensity

Edan Lepucki doesn't expect her next book to be featured by Stephen Colbert, but she's learned a lot from that experience and thinks others can too. Even before she was swept up in a whirlwind of signings and cable television, the publishing experience took her by surprise in its intensity. She says you have to stay focused on whatever work you have to do, whether that's writing the next book or promoting the current one.

"I know this next book won't happen the same way. But I know that I still have to stay focused on the work at hand. It's really easy to lose yourself in the whole publishing experience, even when everything is going well. There were times during that whole *California* blitz where I still had to go back to my hotel room and cry because it was just too intense. It's like you're a lobster without a shell. Suddenly your book is in the world and it's not yours anymore, and you're getting mean reviews on Amazon and Goodreads. So I always tell anyone who's about to publish a book, 'If you have to cry, that's okay. I know this is the best moment of your life, but that doesn't mean it can't simultaneously be a shitty moment.'"

Stay Grounded

The writing life occasionally leads to bursts of attention and praise — but it's important to remember that even if it happens, it won't necessarily happen again. Clara Bensen, who rode a viral sensation to a publishing and movie deal, knows that she needs to stay grounded and not expect that kind of success with every project.

"I know that whatever I do next is not going to be as sensational. I just know and accept that. I can't top it from that perspective, and I don't want to. Whatever I do next will have to be carried by my skill, so that's what I'm focused on developing."

Know Your Work

Zetta Elliott is a staunch critic of traditional publishing and the choices it makes in regard to authors of color. She firmly believes that major publishers need radical change, not incremental change, not just bringing in one person on staff to represent people of color. That seems to be the typical approach right now, and she argues that person "tends to just have to assimilate into the dominant culture in order to survive. So they end up reproducing the same dysfunction and bias."

But that doesn't mean Zetta has given up entirely on traditional publishing. She advocates that authors know their own work and do the research and self-advocacy to find the best home for it. "I don't think we have to universally give up on the traditional industry. There are editors out there and books coming out that are making change. I personally have divided my list, and I know which books have a chance of being picked up in traditional publishing. It really comes down to knowing your own work and figuring out where it has a chance of landing."

You Can Always Write Another Book

Edan Lepucki thinks the biggest lesson an aspiring writer could learn from her own path to publication is that you don't have to quit just because you failed. She spent many years writing the manuscript for a book that she knows will likely never see the light of day. But instead of brooding over it, she started in on the next one.

"Even if you spend years writing a book that doesn't sell, you can always write another one, and if that one doesn't sell, you can still write another one. If you keep hearing no and you still keep writing, I think that means you're destined to do it. I know so many people who have given up after they heard some nos. And maybe some people would say I just got lucky. I mean, I fully recognize I was lucky with what happened to me. But I had to work hard to get there. Even if you get lucky, you have to work hard and keeping working hard to make luck happen."

The Next Project Is Just as Hard

It isn't all sundaes and rainbows after you publish your first book. Courtney Maum has learned lessons from her first book, but it doesn't make writing the second one any easier. In some ways she expected it to be easier, which has made it all the harder. So she says expect it to continue to be hard, and you won't be shaken when it is.

"I've learned that it gets harder in some ways, not easier. Really. I'm surprised at how difficult the second book is. When it is your first book, you do it all alone in your room and it's all yours. With the second book, it's different. Now other players have a vested interest in what I'm doing, and in many ways I'm grateful for all that, but you also start to internalize that as a pressure."

Start the Next Project

While his memoir was cycling through the publishing gears, Brian started planning out his next project, *The River Signal*. It was an original episodic radio story written and recorded aboard a paddleboat in collaboration with a series of artists and musicians. When his debut book was out of his hands, he could turn his attention to this project rather than fretting about the status of things he had no control over.

"Publishing is so fast and so slow. There are parts where you are flying through it and have to make so many decisions really quickly. And then long, yawning silences. So one thing I learned was having another project to work on in those silences is really, really important."

Persevere and Have Fun

Writing is hard work, and some of it can be drudgery. But Monona Wali tries to balance two things as she continues to write. First, "have fun as you write." It's hard to remember with pressures and rejections and deadlines that writing can and should be creative expression and fun. Try not to forget that.

And second, she recommends adopting "Persistence" as your motto. "If you want this, you have to put in the work. You have to be persistent. I have known writers who got their first book published very quickly, but then they stopped writing. Publication is a nice dessert, but I think the real game is the writing and the process and the relationships you build along the way.

"Few writers are making a ton of money from their writing, and even fewer are getting famous, so you have to ask yourself, 'Why am I doing this?' It's not that I don't still want those things on some level, I do. But I do think it's important for an aspiring writer to understand and value that they are part of this amazing art form that you can constantly learn from. So if you embrace those two things [fun and persistence], then you'll be in it for the long haul."

Be Nice

There's a lot you can't control. Will you be rejected for years? Will you have a smash best seller and be on the cover of magazines? Those things aren't up to you. But you can control how you treat other people and your fellow writers. Courtney Maum says it may be hard sometimes, but just *be nice*. Writers need support, and being supportive of others whether you've hit it big or hit a wall is always the best choice.

"Don't be false. Don't be mean. Try not to hate other people. You might be hearing all these people say, 'Just got a book deal!' or 'My book just went into its seventh printing,' and you need to be supportive of that even when things are going bad for you. It's so much harder than it sounds, but it is my strongest piece of advice. When you make it, don't be an asshole. When other people make it, don't be an asshole. I've seen people do that in both situations, and really it's so important not to do that or be that."

Embrace Writing as a Lifestyle

Yes, writing can be a career, and Alan Heathcock thinks about the business side often. But fundamentally, he believes that if you're going to be successful at this, you have to come at it as a lifestyle choice, a way of choosing to interact with the world.

"I'm never not a writer. It's something I do because it makes my time on this planet better. It makes me a better father, husband, son, friend, and citizen. It lets me look around the world and take an accounting of the things that I think are beautiful and hopeful and filled with joy, and the things that I think are deeply disturbing and that I want to change."

There is no better way to live if you embrace writing that way, he says. And more important, "you won't get turned sideways into this high-pressure game that you'll want to shrug off. Keep your head space outside of the professional goals; just embrace writing as something core to your life, and everything else can work itself out."

Finish It Anyway

Cynthia Bond recommends that every aspiring writer read Michael Ventura's 1993 essay "The Talent of the Room," originally published in *LA Weekly*. His basic argument is that you can have all the talent in the world, but if you don't have or develop the ability to sit alone in a room and write something, you will never finish. That was a huge lesson in Cynthia's approach, and one she wishes she had considered much earlier in her process.

"It's important to remember that the more important something is in your life purpose, the greater resistance you will face. People often say that writing a book is like giving birth, and that's sometimes true, but the difference is that with a novel you can always opt out. You can put it back in a drawer for forty years and never look at it again. So you need to know and anticipate resistance, know that there will be great pain, know that it will take longer than you think it is going to take, but that you have to keep at it. You're the only one who can finish it! So expect the resistance, and finish it anyway."

It Matters

It has been a joy to profile these eleven gifted and generous authors, but like theirs, my own journey hasn't been easy. I've encountered setbacks and doubt and dismay as I wrote this book. This is also my first book, and since as I write this it isn't yet published, I'm not sure how much advice I'm entitled to give. But if I have some leeway, my advice is this.

Writing matters. Stories matter. That idea you have, that story you want to write—it matters. It can seem pointless, daunting, silly, or trivial, but you should write it anyway. Our world hurts, and I believe that stories are part of the cure. They allow us to laugh, to understand, to experience, to mourn, and to connect. We need them.

You might not think you're good enough, or ready enough, or dedicated enough. You might think all the odds are stacked against you—I sure did when I began to pursue this idea—but since I believe stories matter, I'll close by quoting from one of my favorites from childhood.

He was told it was crazy, that the odds of successfully navigating an asteroid field were 3720-to-one. But Han Solo flew in anyway. "Never tell me the odds," he said.

You can do it. I can't wait to read it.

Acknowledgments

Open any book and, yes, you hold in your hands the tireless work of an author, but you also hold the hard work, support, and dedication of many generous souls. This book started with a cup of coffee with my wonder agent, Dawn Frederick. Sometimes I hear somebody question the value of an agent. They haven't seen Dawn's exhausting schedule, dogged effort, and fierce devotion to her authors. Dawn, I'm grateful to have you in my corner.

On the editorial side of things, I'm blessed to have found and worked with Mary Laur and her colleagues at the University of Chicago Press. Her ideas and revisions helped reshape this book into something eminently better. I've long wondered why editors don't get their names on the cover with the author. So I'll lodge my protest here and say that she deserves it.

To the authors, agents, editors, and others who agreed to take part in this book, having never known or met me, thank you. I'm ever grateful for your gifts of time and wisdom. Any wisdom in these pages is yours, any errors or missteps, mine.

To the supportive friends along this journey, my endless thanks. In particular to the past and present colleagues, interns, teachers, students, authors, and volunteers at the Loft—your curiosity, love of lit, and passion for baked goods serves as the bedrock for this book. I also wouldn't be in the position I am in without some wonderful teachers who taught me a deep love of reading and writing. To Richard Latham, Richard Meacock, Maureen Conway, Marilyn Shardlow, Margery Smith, Robert Grunst, Sidney Wade, William Logan, and Michael Hoffman, thank you. I'd also like to specifically thank the friends who make it all worthwhile, Jim, Kristine, Becky, Jon, Ross, Chessa, Ryan, Tina, Madhurima, Kris, Kevin, Ina, Justin, Kate, Nate, Josh, Mat, Rachel, Austin, Aaron, Jess, David, Marin, Jim, Abby, Charles, Michael, Suzanne, Anna, Sasha, Sam, Ben, Dwight, Per, Paul, Martin, Thomas, Carmen, Kerstin, and many more whom I just don't have the space to include.

To my family, the Bayntons (especially Lin and Bob), the Barwicks, the Joneses, the Millers, the Watts, the Yaremas, the Hardins, the Reids, and in particular my parents David and Julie: your love, your kindness, your laughter, your support can never be measured or repaid. Thank you.

To my brother Nick, I miss you every day.

Finally, to Dannah: You never questioned this little quest, even when the seas got pretty rough. The sacrifices, the space to write, the hours of editorial help, the talking me down, the talking me up, and the belief in me all the while — for that and so much more, thank you. I love you, and I owe you a date night.

Appendix: The Complete Lineup

Clara Bensen, *No Baggage: A Minimalist Tale of Love & Wandering*

No Baggage is a travel memoir that rose out of a viral *Salon* article titled "The Craziest OKCupid Date Ever." The original article explored a baggageless trip across the world with someone she barely knew, and it was one of the first things Clara Bensen had written.

The article has now been read more than five hundred thousand times, and it led to a number of book-deal offers for Clara. When the offers poured in, she wasn't sure she was ready to write a book. "I took one creative writing class in community college," says Clara. "I've long been writing, I'd published a little bit on a personal website, but that *Salon* article was my first publication ever."

But the viral sensation of her story opened a lot of doors, and soon Clara had an agent, a publishing deal, and a movie option, all based on one *Salon* article and a book proposal. That may sound like a dream for any aspiring writer, but it meant Clara had to learn the rules of the publishing world in reverse, which wasn't as wonderful as it sounds.

"Initially people thought it was some kind of stunt or carefully planned marketing ploy. But taking that trip, just like writing this book, was a personal challenge and an adventure. I had to overcome a lot to go on that trip, as I describe in the book, so it was more about just taking a next step. I did not go into it thinking 'This will make a great book.'"

Clara completed *No Baggage* in eight months. It was published by Running Press, a member of the Perseus Books Group, in 2016. It was edited by Jennifer Kasius and represented by Stacy Testa of Writers House.

No Baggage received global coverage and reviews after its release. It has been translated into a dozen languages, and the movie was in development at the time of this writing. Clara is working on her next project, a series of social experiments that play with the intersection between madness and society. She continues to travel around the globe with her partner Jeff—without any bags.

Brian Benson, *Going Somewhere: A Bicycle Journey across America*

Going Somewhere is a work of narrative nonfiction—a candid memoir covering a couple on a cross-country bicycle trip. It explores themes of choice, hindsight, possibility, discovery, and relationships. Cheryl Strayed, who helped Brian develop the book, wrote about *Going Somewhere* that it is "as poignant as it is gripping, as hilarious as it is wise. *Going Somewhere* is a tender, sexy, take-it-with-you-everywhere-you-go-until-you've-read-the-last-page beauty of a book."

Brian Benson grew up in northern Wisconsin, "just outside a town with three bars and no stoplights." He attended the University of Wisconsin and never intended to become a writer. After several years of traveling, and odd jobs here and there, Brian and his then-girlfriend Rachel took a bike trip from his childhood home in Wisconsin to Portland, Oregon.

When he set out for the trip, Brian hadn't once considered writing about it. In the first chapter of *Going Somewhere*, he explains that he wanted to go on the trip to find a sense of direction—"some sense that by going somewhere I was going somewhere." So he cataloged the trip in his journal—the weary bodies and bikes, the many friendly and terrifying chance encounters, the fierce winds and brutal heat, and the changing meaning of the future for each of them. As they neared Portland and the end, Brian started to consider writing a book based on his trip journal.

He had some journalism and academic writing experience but had done almost no creative writing when he set out to write the book. From that first impulse to the day it came out, it took more than five years for Brian to make *Going Somewhere* a reality. He admits to some big gaps along the way when he shelved the project.

Brian points to a number of varied influences on his writing, in particular his close work with Karen Karbo and Cheryl Strayed in a writing program in Portland. But during his trip he was primarily reading two books, *You Shall Know Our Velocity* by Dave Eggers and *The God of Small Things* by Arundhati Roy. He says those books, for different reasons, helped shape his plan to write his own book. Eggers's novel, which is "so much about privilege and guilt and choice," crystallized some of Brian's own thoughts about his journey. He was particularly taken with how Eggers was able to turn abstract ideas into a specific story. Roy's influence was less about the story and more about the language. Maybe more than when reading any other writer, he says, "when I read her work, I want to put the book down all the time and just start writing."

Going Somewhere was published by Plume, an imprint of Penguin Random House, in 2014. It was edited by Denise Roy and represented by David Forrer of Inkwell Management Literary Agency.

Since coming out, *Going Somewhere* was selected as a Powell's New Favorite and a Multnomah County Library selection. It has been listed in several "best of" travel and biking book lists. In 2015, a year after *Going Somewhere*'s release, Brian coproduced *The River Signal*, a radio drama written and recorded during a trip down the Mississippi River. He continues to teach creative writing at the center that helped him find his sea legs as a writer, the Attic Institute in Portland, and he is now at work on a second book. This time he's trying his hand at a novel.

Cynthia Bond, *Ruby*

Ruby is a work of literary fiction and a *New York Times* best seller, described in promotion as an "epic, unforgettable story of a man determined to protect the woman he loves from the town desperate to destroy her." The story weaves together multiple narrative threads and covers challenging themes of human trafficking, sexual violence, mental health, and racism.

Ruby's author, Cynthia Bond, was born in East Texas but spent much of her childhood in Lawrence, Kansas, where her father was a literature and theater professor. As a young girl, she was fortunate enough to meet Gwendolyn Brooks, Sonia Sanchez, Nikki Giovanni, and Maya Angelou, and each made an impression on her work in adulthood.

By the time she left home for college, she'd been exposed to a lot of writing. She recalls the massive stacks of books strewn around the house. But she did not intend to be a novelist; when she left for college, she had her eye on a degree in journalism.

Cynthia worked in journalism for a while, but memories of her dad's theater work pulled her in another direction—acting. "As a young girl I'd watch him, sit in the back of the auditorium while he was directing plays, and then we'd go home and just talk about structure and the arc of the characters," she says.

So she returned to school and pursued a life in theater. After several years Cynthia shifted yet again and moved into social work, mostly working with at-risk and runaway youth. Many years later—still working with these populations and after personal struggles of her own—Cynthia found herself in a community writing class, where she started what would become her first novel, *Ruby*.

Cynthia says all three of her career stops helped inform and propel her work. "In journalism school, I learned about crafting a story in a succinct manner. In acting school, I played a lot of characters in really good plays. So I learned about exploring the arc of characters, the twists and turns and rise and fall in those stories. And then in my work with youth, I lived it. The stories in this book needed to be told because there are so many children on this earth who are going through the unimaginable. And I really sometimes believe that we are unaware that we are living through a genocide of children. People don't see it, they don't know it, they're unaware of it. But kids are being killed, they're being chained to beds, given drugs to make them comply, being thrown out of their homes because they're gay or transgender. So those stories are just a part of me now, and I needed to try to tell them."

From the initial impulse to write it to the day it came out, *Ruby* took Cynthia Bond fifteen years to complete. *Ruby* was published by Hogarth, an imprint of Penguin Random House, in 2014. It was edited by Lindsay Sagnette and represented by Nicole Aragi of Aragi, Inc.

Ruby was a *New York Times* best seller, an Oprah's Book Club 2.0 selection, and a finalist for the PEN / Robert W. Bingham Prize. It reached numerous best-seller lists and has been translated into many languages. At the time of this writing, Cynthia Bond is working on the second book in the Ruby trilogy.

Delilah Dawson, *Wicked as They Come*

Wicked as They Come blends a number of genres including fantasy, paranormal, steampunk, and romance. It is the story of a woman who finds herself swept into and ultimately trapped in a surreal, faraway world full of Blud-creatures and Bludmen.

Wicked as They Come was written by Atlanta's Delilah Dawson. She had never intended to become a writer; in her youth she didn't really think it was possible. While she was growing up, she says, you couldn't just type "how to get published" into Google and find thousands of answers. "So being an author was like being a magical being. I didn't even think it was possible, and so I didn't write my first book until I was thirty-two."

Her first book wasn't *Wicked as They Come*, which was actually her third completed manuscript. "The first book I wrote was so totally wretched that I use the first chapter in classes. I show it and say, 'Look, even if you write this poorly, you can still get published one day.' By the time I had the idea for *Wicked as They Come*, I knew I could write and finish a book. If I hadn't tried to write those others, I don't think I would've had the skills to turn it into a book."

From idea to landing on the shelf, *Wicked as They Come* took two years to become reality. It was published by Pocket Books, a division of Simon & Schuster, in 2012. It was edited by Abby Zidle and represented by Kate McKean of Morhaim Literary.

Wicked as They Come launched a growing and prolific career for Delilah. Since its release, Delilah has published dozens of stories, e-books, books, and comics, under her own name and two pen names. She has received numerous starred reviews and awards, including RT Book Reviews Steampunk Book of the Year award. She regularly teaches for Lit Reactor.

Zetta Elliott, *Bird*

Bird is a picture book about a boy named Mehkai, better known as Bird to the people who know him. Bird loves to draw and tries to use drawings to cope with the death of his grandfather and with his older brother's drug addiction. Featuring beautiful illustrations from Shadra Strickland, *Bird* tells the story of a young boy coming to terms with real-life issues of addiction and loss. The story has been widely praised for allowing new and more open conversations around mortality and addiction with young children—issues that many small children experience firsthand but don't know how to talk about.

Zetta Elliott wrote *Bird* quickly, in "about a day." But she revisited and revised the manuscript over many years before submitting it. Many publishers and agents told her the book's content was too mature for a picture book. Finally, after persevering through criticism and an industry she views as stacked against writers of color like herself, Zetta submitted it to the Lee & Low New Voices Contest, and the book was awarded first prize.

The prize came with a cash award and the potential for being published by Lee & Low. The book was published traditionally, but not without bumps along the way—enough bumps that Zetta Elliott has now mostly turned to self-publishing.

Between the day she sat down to write it and the day it came out, *Bird* took about five years to become reality. It was published by Lee & Low Books in 2008. After its release, *Bird* received numerous starred reviews and was listed on many best-children's-books-of-the-year lists. It won the Ezra Jack Keats Book Award, the Paterson Prize for Books for Young People, and a Coretta Scott King Award, and was named an ALA Notable Children's Book.

As of this writing, Zetta Elliott has now published eighteen books for children, four books for teens, two books for adults, and three plays. She has self-published most of those works and continues to advocate for writers of color in publishing.

Alan Heathcock, *Volt*

Volt is a collection of linked short stories, all taking place in a fictional small town named Krafton. The stories connect lives torn apart—and sometimes sewn back together—by tragedy, violence, and injustice.

The collection originated as two failed novel attempts by Alan after his MFA program. "In graduate school I wrote short stories because that's what people do, but in my mind I really wanted to be a novelist. So I had these novel ideas, but I didn't know how to write a novel."

One of the key elements of the stories is the town of Krafton, and Alan wanted it to feel like a place that could be anywhere in

America. He avoided setting the stories somewhere specific because he found that readers attach a secondary layer of meaning based on their knowledge of an existing place, and he didn't want that. "Having traveled a lot throughout this country, I know there is a kind of homogeneity to small towns. There are differences in flora and fauna and accents and verbiage, but I was more interested in finding a template that just seemed like America."

With that place firmly in his mind, he started dissecting his two failed novels and identifying the most powerful sections and stories from them. As Alan puts it, those sections had one thing in common: the muck. Moments of terror, grief, and injustice — "volt moments," as he also calls them — that ripple through the characters and the town, changing them forever. So he focused on those, revising some stories and writing some new ones until he had the complete collection for *Volt*.

All told, *Volt* took about ten years to come into existence. It was published by Graywolf Press in 2011. The collection was edited by Fiona McCrae and represented by Sarah Burnes of the Gernert Company.

When *Volt* came out it was named a Best Book of 2011 by *Publishers Weekly*, *Shelf Awareness*, *GQ*, *Salon*, *Book Page*, the *Plain Dealer* (Cleveland), and the *Chicago Tribune*. Alan won the prestigious Whiting Award for *Volt*, and the singer-songwriter Chad Summerville released an album of songs based on the book. Alan now teaches creative writing at Boise State University; he has published a number of short stories since *Volt*'s release.

Edan Lepucki, *California*

California is a dystopian novel, or as Edan Lepucki puts it, "a post-apocalyptic domestic drama." It follows a husband and wife, in shifting points of view, across an apocalyptic California. Not only must this couple figure out the newly devastated world, but they must also balance their reliance on each other with the secrets they continue to keep from each other.

Edan Lepucki began *California* because she heard from numerous agents and editors that her first novel manuscript, which she had spent many years writing, was not going to sell. At the time, she had completed her MFA degree from the Iowa Writers' Workshop and she was teaching in and around Los Angeles. Besides the novel that never got off the ground, Edan had published some short stories and was a frequent contributor to *The Millions*.

California is the novel that Stephen Colbert held up in front of his *Colbert Report* audience in 2014 and instructed them to buy from Powell's Books to protest the Amazon-Hachette dispute. That TV moment helped propel Edan's debut novel to best-seller lists.

The book took four years from the moment she started it to the moment it landed on shelves, and in thousands of readers' mailboxes through their Powell's orders. It was published by Little, Brown, an imprint of Hachette, in 2014. *California* was edited by Allie Sommer and represented by Erin Hosier at Dunow, Carlson, and Lerner.

California debuted at number 3 on the *New York Times* Best Sellers List and has been number 1 on the *Los Angeles Times* and *San Francisco Chronicle* best-sellers lists. It also was listed on the IndieBound and *Publishers Weekly* Bestsellers Lists. Edan's second novel, *Woman No. 17*, released in 2017.

Rebecca Makkai, *The Borrower*

The Borrower is a novel of literary fiction which Pulitzer Prize winner Richard Russo described as "smart and engaging and learned and funny and moving." It's the story of a school librarian who starts by innocently trying to sneak books past an overbearing and censoring mother to a child who needs them. But the more she learns about the child and his home life, the more she wants to help, and in a moment of desperation, they leave together on a road trip across the country.

Although the relationship is entirely nonsexual, the story echoes back to Nabokov's *Lolita*; with a mix of humor and empathy, it explores themes of permission, parenting, boundaries, secrets, children's literature, homosexuality, and discovery.

The Borrower was written by Chicago-based author Rebecca Makkai. More than ten years passed from the moment she had the idea to the day *The Borrower* came out. In the interim Rebecca had become one of the nation's most respected short-story writers, appearing in *Best American Short Stories* four years in a row.

Before these accomplishments, Rebecca had often felt she wasn't yet ready to pull off a novel, which led her to set it aside for long periods of time.

Rebecca says she was influenced by many things you would expect, based on the story's themes and plot: *Lolita, Huckleberry Finn, The Wizard of Oz,* and *Catcher in the Rye.* But one surprising influence is a 1995 Cameron Diaz movie called *The Last Supper.* It's a black comedy in which liberal graduate students invite offensive bullies over for dinner and poison them. Rebecca says, "They ultimately get this Rush Limbaugh figure over for dinner, but he begins to undercut a lot of what they thought about him, and it calls into question everything they've done, their entire belief system."

Although the movie's story is completely different from her own, Rebecca says the movie was frequently on her mind when she began writing the story. "My character was going to have to change internally pretty dramatically. If she was going to set out thinking that taking Ian was the right thing to do, I knew she was going to have to have all that called into question by the end. A story like this needs to shake a character's foundation."

The Borrower was published by Viking, an imprint of Penguin Random House, in 2011. It was edited by Alexis Washam and represented by Nicole Aragi of Aragi, Inc.

The Borrower was selected as an Indie Next Pick, was named to a number of "best of" lists for debut fiction, and has been translated into eight languages. Since its release Rebecca Makkai has won an NEA Fellowship, published two more widely acclaimed books, and taught at the Iowa Writers' Workshop, Tin House, and Northwestern University.

Courtney Maum, *I Am Having So Much Fun Here without You*

I Am Having So Much Fun Here without You is a literary novel set in Paris. It is intentionally not a typical Paris story. This story splits between moments of dark comedy and piercing observation — it revolves around a man whose lover recently left him and whose wife found out. The apparent positives in his life — the romance of Paris, the successful art career, the loving family — are just illusions, and we follow this man as he tries to put his life back together.

One of the strengths (or, for some, weaknesses) of this book is that the main protagonist is complicated and often unlikable. Some readers and critics negatively focused on his likability in reviews. More reviews, however, praised Courtney Maum's ability to make the reader empathize with a challenging character. In addition to the weighty topic, Courtney's book is frequently praised for the amount of humor it delivers.

I Am Having So Much Fun Here without You was almost abandoned permanently. Courtney literally stuffed the manuscript in a box for ten years before returning to it. "I certainly never had any dreams of it seeing the light of day. Nor did I think about self-publishing it, which I have done with other work. I self-published a collection of short stories for the fun of it so I could have something to hand out without having to go through the spiral of rejection again. But this novel — it was just going to stay in that box."

But it didn't. As a result of one conversation, Courtney returned to the manuscript and rewrote the entire novel. By that time she had three other novel-length manuscripts, two of which she also never intended to seek publication for. But that much writing experience meant Courtney wasn't afraid to begin rewriting *I Am Having So Much Fun Here without You* years after she'd abandoned the project. "I wasn't frightened or daunted at all by the idea of this novel. By then I'd already written so much."

More than twelve years passed between the time Courtney had the idea for *I Am Having So Much Fun Here without You* and the day it landed on shelves in 2014. It was published by Touchstone, an imprint of Simon & Schuster. It was edited by Sally Kim and represented by Rebecca Gradinger of Fletcher and Company.

Since it came out, *I Am Having So Much Fun Here without You* has been reviewed widely including in *Vogue*, *People*, the *New York Times*, the *Washington Post*, the *Wall Street Journal*, *O, The Oprah Magazine*, and *Flavorwire*. It was featured on several best-debut-books-of-the-year lists in 2014 and in featured-picks lists on IndieNext, Amazon, and Apple. It has been translated into multiple languages. Courtney's second novel, *Touch*, released in 2017.

Eric Smith, *Inked*

Inked is a young adult fantasy novel about a young man who rebels just before his inking, which in this world means the application of magical tattoos that determine one's fate in society.

When Eric wrote *Inked* he was also working on a book for Quirk Books, where he worked. So Eric split his time between writing *Inked* and writing *The Geek's Guide to Dating*. With a full-time publishing job and two books to write, Eric had to be very disciplined with his time.

Eric points to the video game series Final Fantasy, in addition to some well-known YA fantasy works, as a major influence on *Inked*. He says playing the game feels like playing inside a novel, and he wanted to try to capture that feeling in his own book.

Inked was published in 2015 by Bloomsbury Spark, a young adult digital publishing imprint of Bloomsbury Publishing. It was edited by Meredith Rich and represented by Dawn Frederick of Red Sofa Literary.

For his book launch Eric helped facilitate a theme song written by the band Blue of Colors, and his book has been highlighted in a variety of publications. A second book in the Inked series, titled *Branded*, was published in 2016.

Monona Wali, *My Blue Skin Lover*

My Blue Skin Lover is a magical-realism novel about a married woman who is growing weary of the pressures on her life: the clinical, data-driven focus of her PhD advisor, the materialism of her husband's corporate ladder climbing, and the loneliness and frenetic pace of living in New York City. She meets the god Shiva by chance, and they ultimately have a love affair. The book explores themes of materialism, marriage, friendship, self-discovery, and spirituality.

Monona Wali wrote the book with the intention of publishing it in the traditional way, but after a few missteps, including paying for editorial advice that set her work back and an agent who abandoned her, she had mostly given up on publishing the story at all. But soon people in Monona's life pushed her to explore other options. That push led her to revise and self-publish the book in 2014 through Blue Jay Ink, nearly four years after she started it.

My Blue Skin Lover wasn't the first thing Monona had written, however. She has published numerous short stories and written and edited a 1991 award-winning documentary called *María's Story*. She turned to working on novels only about a decade ago. An early manuscript has been left in a drawer, and she freely admits, "I really didn't know what I was doing." Yet that failed novel helped pave the way for her work on *My Blue Skin Lover*.

My Blue Skin Lover came out and mostly sold locally, through Monona's connections and circles. It then gained sales and reviews after winning Independent Book Publishers' 2015 IPPY Award for Best Multicultural Fiction, one of the most influential and respected award series for self-published books. Monona Wali continues to teach creative writing and is working on her next novel.

Notes

The Ignored Question

1. Lisa Cron, *Wired for Story: The Writer's Guide to Using Brain Science to Hook Readers from the Very First Sentence* (New York: Ten Speed Press, 2012).
2. Aristotle, *Poetics*, trans. Malcolm Heath (London; New York: Penguin Classics, 1997).
3. Confucius, *The Analects*, trans. D. C. Lau (Harmondsworth, UK: Penguin Classics, 1998).
4. George Orwell, *Why I Write* (New York: Penguin Books, 2005).
5. Joan Didion, "Why I Write," *New York Times Magazine*, December 5, 1976, http://www.idiom.com/~rick/html/why_i_write.htm.
6. Archibald MacLeish, *Collected Poems 1917–1982* (Boston: Houghton Mifflin, 1985), https://www.poetryfoundation.org/poetrymagazine/poems/detail /17168.
7. Octavia Butler, "'Devil Girl From Mars': Why I Write Science Fiction," http:// web.mit.edu/comm-forum/papers/butler.html, accessed September 24, 2016.
8. Meredith Maran, ed., *Why We Write: 20 Acclaimed Authors on How and Why They Do What They Do* (New York: Plume, 2013).
9. Cron, *Wired for Story*.

Chapter 1

1. Patrick Rothfuss, "Pep Talk from Patrick Rothfuss," National Novel Writing Month, 2013, http://nanowrimo.org/pep-talks/patrick-rothfuss.
2. Neil Gaiman, "Where Do You Get Your Ideas?," 1997, http://www.neilgaiman .com/Cool_Stuff/Essays/Essays_By_Neil/Where_do_you_get_your _ideas%3F.
3. Clara Bensen, "The Craziest OkCupid Date Ever," *Salon.com*, November 11, 2013, http://www.salon.com/2013/11/12/the_craziest_okcupid_date_ever/.

Chapter 3

1. Franz Kafka, *Letters to Milena*, trans. Philip Boehm (New York: Schocken, 2015).

Chapter 4

1. Vivian Gornick, *The Situation and the Story: The Art of Personal Narrative* (New York: Farrar, Straus and Giroux, 2002).
2. Delilah Dawson, "25 Humpalicious Steps for Writing Your First Sex Scene," *Terribleminds*, blog hosted by Chuck Wendig, April 30, 2013, http:// terribleminds.com/ramble/2013/04/30/25-humpalicious-steps-for-writing -your-first-sex-scene-by-delilah-s-dawson-author-of-wicked-as-she-wants/.
3. Sven Birkerts, *The Art of Time in Memoir: Then, Again* (Saint Paul, MN: Graywolf Press, 2007).
4. Sherry Ellis, *Now Write!: Fiction Writing Exercises from Today's Best Writers and Teachers* (New York: TarcherPerigee, 2006).

Chapter 5

1. W. K. Wimsatt, *The Verbal Icon: Studies in the Meaning of Poetry* (Lexington: University Press of Kentucky, 1954).
2. Roland Barthes, *Image-Music-Text*, trans. Stephen Heath (New York: Hill and Wang, 1978).
3. Chuck Wendig, "25 Ways To Plot, Plan and Prep Your Story," *Terrible Minds*, blog, 2015, http://terribleminds.com/ramble/2011/09/14/25-ways-to-plot -plan-and-prep-your-story/.

Chapter 6

1. Lawrence Grobel, *Conversations with Capote* (New York: Plume, 1986).
2. Vladimir Nabokov, *Speak, Memory: An Autobiography Revisited* 2nd ed. (New York: Vintage, 1989).
3. Jeanne McCulloch and Mona Simpson, "Alice Munro, The Art of Fiction No. 137," *Paris Review*, Summer 1994, http://www.theparisreview.org/interviews/1791/the-art-of-fiction-no-137-alice-munro.
4. Sir Arthur Quiller-Couch, *On the Art of Writing* (Mineola, NY: Dover, 2006).

Chapter 7

1. Jane Hu, "Very Recent History: The 'Slush Pile,'" *The Awl*, July 12, 2010, https://theawl.com/very-recent-history-the-slush-pile-423d6034dda2.
2. Edan Lepucki, "Reasons Not to Self-Publish in 2011–2012: A List," *The Millions*, November 29, 2011, http://www.themillions.com/2011/11/reasons-not-to-self-publish-in-2011-2012-a-list.html.

Index

Academy of Achievement, 45
Adventures of Huckleberry Finn, The
   (Twain), 84, 94, 206
agents, 1–3, 9, 19, 42–43, 54, 58, 93, 95–
   97, 100–101, 111–12, 131, 138, 140–41,
   143–45, 148, 151–53, 156–57, 170,
   180; building relationships, 127–29;
   publishing history and, 124–26;
   querying, 93, 116–17, 119–29, 187–
   88; responses from, 117–19; slush
   pile / inbox, 119–24
ALA Notable Children's Book, 203
Alexie, Sherman, 168, 173
Almond, Steve, 114
Amazon, 154, 165–67, 173, 188, 205
American Psycho (Ellis), 67
Angelou, Maya, 29, 48, 123, 200
Aragi, Nicole, 2–3, 100–101, 122–24,
   151–52, 159, 170, 180, 201
Armstrong, Lance, 155
Around the World in Eighty Days
   (Verne), 31

Artful Edit, The (Bell), 114
Art of Description, The (Doty), 77
Art of Intimacy, The (D'Erasmo), 77
Art of Subtext, The (Baxter), 77
Art of Time in Memoir, The (Birkerts),
   40, 73–74, 77
Atlantic, 28–29, 142
Attic, 53, 78, 199–200; the Atheneum,
   53–54, 102, 128, 185
Atwood, Margaret, 44
authenticity in writing, 66–68

Baldacci, David, 6
Baldwin, James, 29; "The Creative
   Process," 44
Barthes, Roland, "La mort de l'auteur,"
   79
Baxter, Charles, 77
Beardsley, Monroe, 79
Bell, Susan, 114
Bensen, Clara, 165–66, 176, 183–84,
   188–89, 197–98; agent, 1, 42–43, 54,

Bensen, Clara (*continued*)
117–19, 152; authenticity in writing, 66; book launch, 165; book sale, 152; "The Craziest OKCupid Date Ever," 27, 40, 66, 117; deadlines, 85, 138; feedback, 54–55, 103, 172, 174–75; inspiration for *No Baggage*, 26–27; mental health struggles, 26, 40, 66, 73, 85, 118, 175; publicity and promotion, 158–59, 171, 174–75; revisions, 54–55, 73, 103; support network, 54–55, 57; writing process, 40, 42–43, 73–74, 85–86

Benson, Brian, 114, 165–66, 184, 185, 190, 198–200; agent, 1, 111, 127–28, 138, 144–45; authenticity in writing, 66–67; book launch, 164–65; book sale, 155–56; childhood, 17–19; feedback, 101–3, 110–11; inspiration for *Going Somewhere*, 16–18; publicity and promotion, 159, 164–68, 171; rejection, 144–45; revisions, 86, 102–3, 110–11, 155; road trip to Portland, 16–18, 198; sacrifices made to write, 58; setbacks, 138; support network, 53–54, 101–2; theme, 86; writing process, 18, 38, 40, 89–90, 128, 199

Beowulf, 147

Best American Mystery Stories, 125

Best American Short Stories, 15, 41, 124, 125, 206

Bird (Elliott), 2, 75, 132–33, 142, 174, 202–3; awards list, 203; character development, 24, 39, 68, 147; feedback, 56, 104, 142–43; illustrations, 105, 132, 202; inspiration for, 23–24; publicity and promotion, 174; publishers excluding difficult topics, 104–5, 133, 189, 203; race and pub-lishing, 23, 39, 104–5, 133–34, 143, 189, 203; rejection, 142–43, 181; re-vision, 104–5, 203; writing process, 39, 74–75, 186

Bird by Bird (Lamott), 30, 77

Birkerts, Sven, 40, 73

Bloomsbury Publishing, 3, 208

Bloomsbury Spark, 3, 106, 208

Blue Jay Ink, 4, 157, 209

Boise State University, 58, 204

Bond, Cynthia, 2, 115, 134, 176, 185–86, 200–201; agent, 2, 100, 122–23, 151–52; book launch, 145; book sale, 151–52, 154; childhood, 48, 200; feedback, 100–101, 148, 175; inspi-ration for *Ruby*, 22–23; Oprah, 145, 169–70, 175, 201; publicity and pro-motion, 159, 169, 175; race and pub-lishing, 134; revisions, 100–101, 115, 185; setbacks, 145–46, 166; support network, 52, 56; writing process, 41, 84–85, 192–93, 201

book launch, 145, 164–65, 167

Book of Hours (Rilke), 26

Book Page, 204

book publishing: acknowledgments, bio, and head shots, 162; advance release copy, 162; connecting with readers of, 171–76; copyedits and typesetting, 155–56, 161; cover de-sign, 156–58, 162; developmental edits, 161; digital presence, 162; launch, 162, 164–67; manuscript auction, 150–52; orphaned, 156; permissions and fact-checking, 156, 161; planning the next, 176–77; post-sale, 163–77; pre-empt sale, 151–52; publicity and promotion, 155, 158–62, 167–71; reviews, 57, 137–49, 165–67, 170–71, 173, 188;

sale of, 150–54; sales numbers, 166–67; steps from sale to release, 154–58; what to expect, 161–62

BookRiot, 14

Borrower, The (Makkai), 3, 15–16, 41, 57, 175, 205–6; book sale, 150–51, 155; character development, 64–65, 68, 94, 175–76, 206; deadlines, 155; feedback, 175–76; inspiration for, 15–16; narrative, 34; perseverance, 149, 180; publication credits, 124–26; publicity and promotion, 159, 170–71; revisions, 93–95, 99, 123; sacrifices made to write, 58; setbacks while writing, 138–39; theme and metaphor, 84, 205; writing process used, 33–36, 183, 186

Branded (Smith), 208

Bread Loaf Writers' Conference, 53, 153

Brooklyn Public Library, 174

Brooks, Gwendolyn, 48, 200

Buffy the Vampire Slayer, 24

Burnes, Sarah, 2, 125–26, 153

Butler, Octavia, 44–45; "The Devil Girl from Mars," 6

Bygone Bureau, 14

California (Lepucki), 3, 108, 129, 131, 151, 167–69, 173, 183, 188, 204–5; book launch, 167; book sale, 151; character development, 65–66; Colbert, 18, 168–69, 173, 177, 188, 205; feedback, 51–52, 108, 173–74; flashbacks, 74; inspiration for, 18–20; point of view in, 66–67; publicity and promotion, 167–69, 182, 205; revision, 19, 99–100, 108–9; sacrifices made to write, 58; setbacks, 138–39, 140; theme and

metaphor, 80–81; writing process, 36–37, 39–40, 74

Capote, Truman, 92

Catcher in the Rye (Salinger), 206

Center for Fiction, 78

character development, 24–25, 39, 64–66, 68, 70–71, 75, 94, 98–99, 106–8, 112, 147, 172, 175–76, 206–7

charting: action, 89–90; better stories, 87, 88–89; complications, 90; tension, 90–91; themes, 90; time, 91

Chicago Tribune, 145, 204

City of Night (Rechy), 52

Clark, Stephan Eirik, 168

Colbert, Stephen, 18, 168–70, 173, 177, 188, 205

Colbert Report, The, 168, 205

confidence, 41–42, 44–45, 137, 139, 181

Coretta Scott King Award, 203

craft, 63–78; books about, 77–78; dealing with, 76; educational resources on, 78; finding authenticity, 66–69; format, 72–76; keeping the pages turning, 69–72; resources, 76–78; tone, 72–76

Critique Circle, 62

Critters.org, 62

Cron, Lisa, 7–8, 78

Crusoe, Jim, 53

Dancing with Mrs. Dalloway (Johnson), 31

Danticat, Edwidge, 122

Dawson, Delilah, 2, 176, 179, 182, 201–2; agent, 2, 112, 119–22, 140–41, 143, 148, 156; book launch, 164; book sale, 155–56, 187; character development, 25, 65, 70–71, 172; childhood, 49, 201–2; deadlines, 155–56; feedback, 55–56, 112–13, 143, 171; inspi-

Dawson, Delilah (*continued*)
ration for *Wicked as They Come*,
24–25; perseverance, 179–80, 187;
publicity and promotion, 129, 158;
rejection, 143–46; revision, 113;
setbacks, 140–41; sex scenes, writ-
ing, 55–56, 70; side projects, 148;
support network, 49, 54–57; "25
Humpalicious Steps to Writing
Your First Sex Scene," 70; writing
process, 37–38, 40–41, 43, 86–87
Dead until Dark (Harris), 87
D'Erasmo, Stacey, 77
Díaz, Junot, 28, 122
Didion, Joan, "Why I Write," 6
Doty, Mark, 77
Doyle, Roddy, 45
Dunow, Carlson, and Lerner, 205

Eggers, Dave, 199
Electric Lit, 78
Elements of Style (Strunk &White), 115
Elliott, Zetta, 2, 175, 189, 202–3; authenticity in writing, 68; childhood, 48; editor, 2; feedback, 56,
104, 142–43; inspiration for *Bird*,
23–24; perseverance, 147; publicity
and promotion, 174; race and publishing, 23, 39, 104–5, 133–34, 143,
189, 203; rejection, 142–43, 181, 203;
revision, 104–5; self-publishing,
105, 132–34, 189, 203; support network, 52, 56; writing process, 39,
74–75, 186
Emmons, Cai, "Braiding Time," 74
Epel, Naomi, 29
Ezra Jack Keats Book Award, 203

Facebook, 126, 146, 159, 160
Faulkner, William, 106

feedback, 50–52, 54–56, 59–62; addressing, 100–105; general, 56;
identifying different types of, 51–
52; importance of, 52; online, 62;
professional, 105–13; specific, 56;
toughen up to, 62
Flavorwire, 208
Fletcher and Company, 208
Foer, Jonathan Safran, 122
Forrer, David, 1, 111, 128, 144, 199
Frederick, Dawn, 3, 127, 208

Gabaldon, Diana, 49
Gaiman, Neil, "Where Do You Get
Your Ideas?," 12–13, 16
Galaxy Quest, 181
Geek's Guide to Dating, The (Smith),
127, 181, 208
Gernert Company, 204
Giovanni, Nikki, 48, 200
God of Small Things, The (Roy), 199
Going Somewhere (Benson), 1, 58, 172,
185, 198–99; book launch, 164–65;
book sale, 155–56; feedback, 101–3,
110–11; inspiration for, 16–18; pro-
posal, 111; publicity and promotion,
159, 164–68, 171; rejection, 144–45;
revisions, 86, 144–45; themes, 86,
198; writing process, 18, 38, 40, 89–
90, 128, 199
Goldberg, Natalie, 77
Goloboy, Jennie, 127
Goodreads, 137, 165–67, 173, 188
Gornick, Vivian, 66–67
Gotham Writers Workshop, 53
GQ, 204
Gradinger, Rebecca, 3, 95–99, 126, 157,
208
Graham, Stacey, 127
Graywolf Press, 2, 77, 88, 109, 153, 204

Grub Street, 78
Guardian, 30, 45

Hachette, 3, 167, 168, 205
Hampl, Patricia, 36
Harper's Magazine, 15
Harris, Charlaine, 87
Harvard Review, 125
Hearne, Kevin, 130
Heathcock, Alan, 2, 109, 175, 192, 203–
    4; agent, 2, 125–26, 153; book sale,
    153, 160; feedback, 50–51, 109–10;
    inspiration for Volt, 25–26; perse-
    verance, 146–47, 181; publicity and
    promotion, 160–61, 174; rejection,
    141–42; revisions, 109–10; sacrifices
    made to write, 58; setbacks, 140–
    41; support network, 52, 57; writing
    process, 38–40, 71–72, 87–89
Hemingway, Ernest, 29–30
Hobbit, The (Tolkien), 31
Hogarth, 2, 151, 201
Hosier, Erin, 3, 128–29, 140, 151
Huckleberry Finn (Twain). See Ad-
    ventures of Huckleberry Finn, The
    (Twain)
Huffington Post, 14
Hugo House, 78
Hundred-Year House, The (Makkai),
    36, 93
Huntington Library, 44

I Am Having So Much Fun Here with-
    out You (Maum), 3, 95, 144, 207–8;
    book cover, 157; book launch, 165;
    book sale, 156–57; character devel-
    opment, 68, 98–99, 207; deadlines,
    152; feedback, 50, 67, 144, 172, 175;
    inspiration for, 20–21; rejection,
    144; revision, 67–68, 75–76, 95–99;

114; sacrifices made to write, 58;
    setbacks, 139; theme and metaphor,
    81–83; writing process, 34–35, 75–
    76, 89, 176
ideas for books / inspiration, 12–31;
    accepting imperfection, 30; being
    open to, 31; finding a path, 27–28;
    "finding the butterfly," 30; ignoring
    forgettable, 28–29; "make a pie —
    or something else," 30; out of ideas,
    28–31; persistence in following, 31;
    reading to find, 28; revisiting, 29;
    starting with one true sentence,
    29–30; writing badly to find, 29
If You Want to Write (Ueland), 77
I Know Why the Caged Bird Sings
    (Angelou), 48
Independent Publisher Book Award
    (IPPY), Gold Medal for Multicul-
    tural Fiction, 170, 209
IndieBound, 205
IndieNext, 208
Inked (Smith), 3, 13–15, 103–4, 181, 208;
    book launch, 165; characters, 106–
    8; feedback, 103–4, 106; inspiration
    for, 13–15; prologue, 106–8; rejec-
    tion, 149; revising, 73, 106–8; writ-
    ing process, 32–33, 208
Iowa Writers' Workshop, 43, 51–52,
    205, 206

James, P. D., 45–46
Johnson, Celia Blue, 31
Joyce, James, 146

Kafka, Franz, 47, 52, 59
Karbo, Karen, 53–54, 102, 128, 185,
    199
Kasius, Jennifer, 1, 198
"kill your darlings," 106–7

Kim, Sally, 3, 208
King, Stephen, 29, 77
Kisor, Henry, 52
Kurt Vonnegut: Letters (Vonnegut), 43–44

Lamott, Anne, 30, 77
Last Supper, The (film), 206
LA Weekly, "The Talent of the Room," 192
League of Regrettable Superheroes, The (Morris), 14
Lee & Low Books, 2, 74–75; New Voices contest, 132, 142, 203
Leonard, Elmore, "Ten Rules for Writing Fiction," 45
Lepucki, Edan, 3, 166–67, 177, 183, 189–90, 204–5; agent, 3, 19, 128–29, 140, 151, 187–88; book launch, 167; "The Book of Deeds" draft, 19; book sale, 151; character development, 65–66; feedback, 51–52, 108, 173–74; inspiration for California, 18–20; publicity and promotion, 167–69, 182; revision, 19, 99–100, 108–9; sacrifices made to write, 58; self-publishing, 130–31; setbacks, 138–39, 140; support network, 52, 57; theme and metaphor, 80–82, 90; UCross artist's residency, 19; writing process, 36–37, 39–40, 74
Library of Congress Book Festival, Twelfth Annual, 28
Lighthouse Writers, 78
Literary Review, Bad Sex in Fiction competition, 70
Lit Reactor, 202
Little, Brown, 3, 108, 167, 169, 205
Little Prince, The (Saint-Exupéry), 31
Loft Literary Center, 6, 9–10, 30, 78

Lolita (Nabokov), 84, 94, 205, 206
Los Angeles Times, 205

Maass, Donald, 77
MacArthur Genius Grant, 44
Macleish, Archibald, 6
Mahadevi, Akka, 21–22, 56
Makkai, Rebecca, 3, 141, 205–6; agent, 3, 122–24, 151, 170, 180; authenticity in writing, 65, 68; book sale, 150–51, 155; character development, 64–65, 68, 94, 175–76, 206; childhood, 48; deadlines, 155; feedback, 175–76; inspiration for The Borrower, 15–16; perseverance, 149, 180; publication credits, 124–26; publicity and promotion, 159, 170–71; revisions, 93–95, 99; sacrifices made to write, 58; setbacks, 138–39; support network, 56–57; theme and metaphor, 84; writing process, 33–36, 41, 183, 186
Mantel, Hilary, 30
Maria's Story (film), 21, 209
Maum, Courtney, 3, 141, 184–85, 190, 207–8; agent, 3, 58, 126, 152–53, 157; authenticity in writing, 67–68; book cover, 157; book launch, 165; book sale, 156–57; character development, 68, 98–99, 207; deadlines, 152; feedback, 50, 67, 144, 172, 175; inspiration for I Am Having So Much Fun Here without You, 20–21; perseverance, 152; rejection, 144; revision, 67–68, 75–76, 95–99, 114; sacrifices made to write, 58; self-publishing, 207; setbacks, 139; support network, 53, 191–92; theme and metaphor, 81–83; writing process, 34–35, 75–76, 89, 176

May, Louise, 2
Mayo, Wendell, 146–47
McCarthy, Cormac, 39
McCarthy, Jim, 120
McCrae, Fiona, 2, 88, 109, 153, 204
McKean, Kate, 2, 112–13, 121–22, 140–
    41, 143, 148, 156, 202
McKee, Robert, 77–78
Melena's Jubilee (Elliott), 133
Méliès, Georges, 89
mentors, 52, 53, 54
Mid-American Review, 141
Millions, The, 78, 167, 205; "Reasons
    Not to Self Publish," 130
*Miss Peregrine's Home for Peculiar Chil-
    dren* (Riggs), 14
Morhaim Literary, 202
Motion, Andrew, 46
Moveable Feast, A (Hemingway), 29–
    30
Munro, Alice, 92
My Blue Skin Lover (Wali), 4, 42, 56,
    111–12, 131–32, 170, 209; book cover,
    158; book launch, 165; character
    development, 75, 112; feedback,
    69, 104, 131, 172–73; inspiration for,
    21–22; IPPY award, 170, 209; pub-
    licity and promotion, 160, 170; race
    and publishing, 146; revisions, 99,
    111; self-publishing, 131–32, 154,
    157–58, 170, 209; setbacks, 41–42,
    51, 111–12, 146; Shiva, 21, 83–84, 112,
    172, 209; theme and metaphor, 83–
    84, 209; writing process, 36, 41–42,
    75, 187

Nabokov, Vladimir, 92, 94, 205
National Novel Writing Month
    (NaNoWriMo), 12
NEA Fellowship, 206

Negotiating with the Dead (Atwood),
    44
Nelson, Kristin, 130
Nelson Literary Agency, 130
New England Review, 15
New Yorker, 123
New York Times, 57, 145, 159, 168–69,
    200, 201, 205, 208
No Baggage (Bensen), 42–43, 73, 85–
    86, 152, 197–98; book launch, 165;
    book sale, 152; deadlines, 85, 138;
    feedback, 54–55, 103, 172, 174–75;
    inspiration for, 26–27; narrative,
    74; proposal, 118–19; publicity and
    promotion, 158–59, 171, 174–75; re-
    visions, 54–55, 73, 103; writing pro-
    cess, 40, 42–43, 73–74, 85–86
North American Review, 61
Northwestern University, 206
Now Write!, "Braiding Time"
    (Emmons), 74

On Writing (King), 77
On Writing Well (Zinsser), 115
Oprah Book Club, 169–70, 175, 177, 201
Orwell, George, "Why I Write," 5–6
Outlander (Gabaldon), 49
outlining, 34–35, 39, 72, 89–91, 183

Paris Review, 29
Paterson Prize for Books for Young
    People, 203
Penguin Random House, 1–3, 199, 201,
    206
PEN/Robert W. Bingham Prize, 201
Percy, Benjamin, 153
Perseus Books Group, 1, 198
perseverance, 137–49, 152, 179–83, 187,
    191
Pickett, Jim, 52

Plain Dealer, Cleveland, 204
Plume, 1, 110, 159, 199
Pocket Books, 2, 202
Poets and Writers, 78
Powell's Books, 168, 174, 199, 205
Pride and Prejudice and Zombies (Grahame-Smith), 14
Proust, Marcel, 73
publicity and promotion, 129, 155, 158–62, 164–68, 169, 171, 174–75, 182, 205
Publishers Weekly, 170, 204, 205
publishing paths, 116–36; agents, 1–3, 9, 93, 95–97, 100–101, 111–12, 117–29; control over book, 136; genre, 135; preparing to publish, 150–62; publishing decisions, 134–36; publishing history and, 124–26; purpose in publishing, defining, 135; roadblocks to, 135–36; self-publishing, 116, 129–36, 154, 157–58, 161–62, 170, 189

Quiller-Couch, Arthur, 106–7
Quirk Books, 13–14, 49–50, 127, 208

race and publishing, 23, 39, 104–5, 133–34, 143, 146, 189, 203
Rechy, John, 52
Red Sofa Literary Agency, 127, 208
rejection, 116, 120–22, 141–46, 149, 181, 203
Rekulak, Jason, 127
Remembrance of Things Past (Proust), 73
revision, 92–115; difficulties, 113–15; feedback, addressing, 100–105; feedback, professional, 105–13; finding the core, 93–100; tactics, 114–15

Rich, Meredith, 3, 106, 208
Rilke, Rainer Maria, 26
River Signal, The (Benson), 190, 199
Romance Writers of America, 130
Rothfuss, Patrick, 12
Roy, Arundhati, 199
Roy, Denise, 1, 89–90, 110–11, 199
RT Book Reviews Steampunk Book of the Year award, 202
Ruby (Bond), 2, 84–85, 134, 151, 159, 169–70, 200–201; book launch, 145, 165; book sale, 151–52, 154; feedback, 100–101, 148, 175; inspiration for, 22–23, 201; main character, 22; Oprah, 145, 169–70, 175, 201; publicity and promotion, 159, 169, 175; reviews, 145; revisions, 100–101, 115, 185; support network, 52, 56; writing process, 41, 84–85, 192–93, 201
Running Press, 1, 198
Russo, Richard, 205

sacrifices made to write, 58
Sagnette, Lindsay, 2, 201
Saint-Exupéry, Antoine de, 31
Salon, 204; "The Craziest OKCupid Date Ever," 27, 40, 66, 117, 158, 197
Sanchez, Sonia, 48, 200
San Francisco Chronicle, 205
Santa Monica City College, 53, 132
Scribophile, 61–62
self-publishing, 105, 116, 129–36, 154, 157–58, 161–62, 170, 189; marketing, 130–31, 136; reasons for, 135–36
Serrano, María, 21
setbacks, 41–42, 51, 137–49
Shelf Awareness, 204
Shenandoah, 180
Shipstead, Maggie, 126
Shofner, Amanda, 60

Simon & Schuster, 2–3, 202, 208

Situation and the Story, The (Gornick), 66–67

slush pile, 119–24, 180

Slush Pile Hell, 119

Smith, Eric, 3, 208; agent, 3, 127, 208; book launch, 165; character development, 106–8; feedback, 103–4, 106; inspiration for *Inked*, 13–15; perseverance, 181; rejection, 149; revising, 73, 106–8; support network, 49–50, 52, 59; writing process, 32–33

Smith, Tracy K., 30

Smith, Zadie, 46

social media, 62, 158–59

Solo, Han, 193

Sommer, Allie, 3, 108, 205

Spot the Difference, 63

Stampfel-Volpe, Joanna, 120

Star Wars, 193

Story (McKee), 77–78

storyboarding, 35, 39, 72, 87, 88–89, 90

Strayed, Cheryl, 31, 45, 53–54, 102, 128, 185, 198, 199

Strickland, Shadra, 132, 202

Strunk, William, Jr., 115

Summerville, Chad, 204

support networks, 9, 48–57, 148–49; communicating with people close to you, 60; critique partners, 61; fear of theft, 60–61; finding, 59–92; influences of, 48; seek out book lovers, 61; social network, 61–62; sources of support, 47–62

Sweetness #9 (Clark), 168

Tan, Amy, 45

Terrible Minds, 70

Testa, Stacy, 1, 42–43, 54, 118–19, 138, 152, 158, 198

theme, 79–91; letting the depth emerge, 80–84; planning to find, 84–88

This Won't Take But a Minute, Honey (Almond), 114

Three Slices (Wendig, Hearne, and Dawson), 130

Tin House, 53, 206

Tin House, 15

Tiny Beautiful Things (Strayed), 31

Tolkien, J. R. R., 31

Touch (Maum), 36, 208

Touchstone, 3, 208

Trip to the Moon, A (film), 89

Twain, Mark, 55, 61

Twilight (Meyer), 187

Twitter, 62, 155, 158–59

Ueland, Brenda, 77

University of Florida, 8

University of Kansas, 48

University of Wisconsin, Cooperative Children's Book Center, 143

Ventura, Michael, "The Talent of the Room," 192

Verne, Jules, 31

Viking/Penguin, 3, 151, 206

Virginia Quarterly Review, 125, 142

Vogue, 208

Volt (Heathcock), 2, 58, 87–88, 109, 153, 203–4; book sale, 153, 160; feedback, 50–51, 109–10; inspiration for, 25–26; "Peacekeeper," 125, 142; plot, 71–72; publicity and promotion, 160–61, 174; rejection, 141–42; revisions, 109–10; sacrifices made to write, 58; setbacks while

Volt (Heathcock) (*continued*)
writing, 140–41; "Smoke," 153;
"Stained Freight," 88; writing process, 38–40, 71–72, 87–89, 203–4
Vonnegut, Kurt, 43–44

Wali, Monona, 4, 141, 209; agent, 131;
authenticity in writing, 66; book
cover, 158; book launch, 165; character development, 75, 112; childhood, 48; comfort zone, 180; editor, 51, 111–12; feedback, 69, 104,
131, 172–73; inspiration for *My Blue
Skin Lover*, 21–22; mentor, 52–53;
perseverance, 146, 182–83, 191; publicity and promotion, 160, 170; race
and publishing, 146; revisions, 99,
111; self-publishing, 131–32, 154, 157,
209; setbacks, 41–42, 51, 111–12, 146;
support network, 56, 149; theme
and metaphor, 83–84, 209; writing
process, 36, 41–42, 75, 187
Wallace, David Foster, 155
Wall Street Journal, 15, 208
Walt Disney Studios, 89
Washam, Alexis, 3, 206
Washington & Lee University, 15
Washington Post, 145, 208
Wendig, Chuck, 70, 130; "25 Ways to
Plot, Plan and Prep Your Story,"
86–87
White, E. B., 115
Whitehead, Colson, 122
Whiting Award, 204
Why We Write, 6
Wicked as They Come (Dawson), 2,
49, 55–56, 70–71, 122, 201–2; book
launch, 164; book sale, 155–56, 187;
character development, 25, 65, 70–
71, 172; deadlines, 155–56; feedback,

55–56, 112–13, 143, 171; first draft,
70; inspiration for, 24–25; publicity
and promotion, 129, 158; rejection,
143–46; revision, 113; setbacks,
140–41; sex scenes, writing, 55–56,
70; writing process, 37–38, 40–41,
43, 86–87
Wild (Strayed), 53
William Shakespeare's Star Wars Trilogy
(Doescher), 14
Wimsatt, William, 79
Winfrey, Oprah, 145, 169, 175, 177, 201;
magazine, 208
Wired for Story (Cron), 7–8, 78
Wizard of Oz, The (Baum), 84, 206
Woman No. 17 (Lepucki), 205
World Trade Center, 23
Write Life, The, 60
writer's block, 29
Writers' Block, 30
Writer's Center, 78
Writer's Digest, 78, 187
Writers Dreaming (Epel), 29
Writers House, 42, 118, 158, 198
Writers' League of Texas, 78
writers of color, 133–34, 143, 145, 189,
203
Writer Unboxed, 78
writing, why we write, 5–7, 149, 193
Writing Down the Bones (Goldberg),
77
writing process, 32–46; being open to,
44; blended approach, 37–39; experimenting with, 43–46; finding a
process, 39–43; finding reasons to
write, 45; hundred-page outpour,
36–37; letting the basics arrange
themselves, 43–44; organic approach, 36–37, 39, 100; outlining,
34–35, 39, 72, 89–91, 183; planned

approach, 33–36; protecting, 45–46; research, 40; spreadsheets, 86–87; stamina, 44; storyboarding, 35, 39, 72, 87, 88–89, 90; stubbornness and, 45
Writing the Breakout Novel (Maass), 77
Writing Workshops Los Angeles, 18, 40, 78

Yeats, William Butler, 30
Young, Abe Louise, 54–55, 103
You Shall Know Our Velocity (Eggers), 199
YouTube, 68

Zidle, Abby, 2, 202
Zinsser, William, 115